How to search the World Wide Web efficiently

by

John Shelley

BERNARD BABANI (publishing) LTD
THE GRAMPIANS
SHEPHERDS BUSH ROAD
LONDON W6 7NF
ENGLAND

PLEASE NOTE

Although every care has been taken with the production of this book to ensure that any projects, designs, modifications and/or programs, etc., contained herewith, operate in a correct and safe manner and also that any components specified are normally available in Great Britain, the Publishers and Author(s) do not accept responsibility in any way for the failure (including fault in design) of any project, design, modification or program to work correctly or to cause damage to any equipment that it may be connected to or used in conjunction with, or in respect of any other damage or injury that may be so caused, nor do the Publishers accept responsibility in any way for the failure to obtain specified components.

Notice is also given that if equipment that is still under warranty is modified in any way or used or connected with home-built equipment then that warranty may be void.

© 1998 BERNARD BABANI (publishing) LTD

First Published – September 1998
Reprinted – April 1999

British Library Cataloguing in Publication Data:
A catalogue record for this book is available from the British Library

ISBN 0 85934 453 3

Cover Design by Gregor Arthur
Cover illustration by Adam Willis
Printed and bound in Great Britain by Cox & Wyman Ltd, Reading

Preface

Finding information when needed has always been the key to success. There are many sources available but the Internet and the World Wide Web (WWW) are the latest technologies.

It is clear that more and more people are finding it necessary to use the Web to find information related to their own disciplines. However, a great deal of time is being wasted and frustration caused because they do not have the skills required to find what they are looking for efficiently.

Many are bewildered and confused by the number of different search tools available. Frustrated because they cannot find what they are looking for, overwhelmed by the sheer volume of information provided. There is an art or skill in being able to find what is needed. This book will help you find what you want more efficiently and effectively, explain how search engines work, introduce some of the latest search tools and answer some of the questions we all ask:

Why do I get 160,000 search results, many more than I can cope with?

How can I reduce this number to a more relevant and manageable set of results?

What is the reasoning behind the order in which search tools lists results?

How do search tools decide which pages should come at the top of the list?

Why are there duplicate web pages?

How do I decide which search tool is the 'best' - Yahoo!, InfoSeek, Excite, WebCrawler?

What is the difference, if any, between the various search tools?

Why does one search tool produce a different set of results to another?

How can I improve my searching techniques?

How should I enter search keywords and terms?

How can I find someone's e-mail address?

How can I restrict my search for jobs to the UK?

How can I prevent my children finding porn, hate speech, drugs and alcohol on the Internet?

How is information collected by the search tools?

Is the information up-to-date?

Who Needs to Know?

The Web is becoming a necessary technology for many people in their everyday working life: researchers and research assistants from many disciplines such as law, medicine, politics, physics. Lecturers and teachers, their students and pupils need to glean material for their projects. Not least, the Web is fast becoming a major tool for *distance learning*.

In business, apart from the obvious requirement for information relating to stocks and shares, staff need to find train and air time tables, to book seats and accommodation in hotels, from their offices. They would also like to know the weather conditions in the places they visit.

Staff at all levels are being sent on courses to learn how to find information more efficiently, to make the right choice of search tool, how to narrow the thousands of results to the few that they really want.

Web authors and Web masters need to know how to improve the chances of their pages and sites reaching the outside world.

Then, of course, there are the home and leisure users who wish to pursue hobbies, news, entertainment, jobs, tourist information, and so on. On the other hand, parents and teachers wish to prevent their children from being exposed to pornography, hate speech, drugs and alcohol abuse.

There is no quick solution. What is required is some knowledge, some time and effort spent in learning the techniques of searching and keeping up to date with developments. It was only after investing quite some time in the above that I found the Web to be of any practical value to me.

This text will provide you with all the knowledge required to become a more effective Web user.

I would like to thank Mari-Elena Shelley for reading this text and making many helpful comments prior to its publication, including the following:

> ".. an easy and enjoyable read, written in a friendly, conversational language and of immediate practical use."

> "A *must* for any Internet user, personal or professional. This text makes finding your way around much less intimidating and confusing."

I would also like to thank the following organisations for their permission to use screen shots of their web pages in this text:

> CMP Media Inc.: (publisher of *TechWeb*). AltaVista: (COMPAQ, AltaVista and the AltaVista logo are trademarks or servicemarks of Compaq Corporation. Used with permission). Netscape Communications Corporation, Excite, Microsoft, Northern Light, LookSmart, Encyclopædia Britannica, Inc. Ask Jeeves, Inc.: (the brainchild of David Warthen and its founder).

> Screen shots of the above organisations, where used, have not been modified in any way and their relevant trademarks, logos are copyright material. Their URLs are to be found in Chapter 10 of this book.

About the Author

John Shelley took his postgraduate Diploma and, later, his Masters degree in Computing at Imperial College, London, where he has worked as a lecturer in the Centre for Computing Services for over twenty-five years, providing training in programming, operating systems, Web design, HTML and a wide range of application packages.

He has been Chief Examiner since 1982 for the Oxford Local Delegacy in Computer Studies for their GCE O-level examinations, Senior Examiner for the SEG GCSE Computer Studies (now both defunct) and, at the time of writing, Chief Examiner for O-level Computer Studies for Overseas candidates. Yes! such an examination still exists beyond these shores.

He has written over twelve other books on computing. This is his latest text which he hopes will prove useful to those who need to find information using the World Wide Web.

He would like to dedicate this book to two friends of his:

Fritz   &   Tabitha

Trademarks

Microsoft, MS-DOS, Internet Assistant, Internet Explorer, MNS are registered trademarks of Microsoft Corporation.

Alexa, AltaVista, Amnesi, AOL, AOL NetFind, AskJeeves, AskJeeves for Kids, AT&T, Berkeley University, Billboard Music Information Search, Businesses UK, CMP Media Inc., Companies House, CompuServe, Cyber Patrol, CyberSitter, Deja News, Deutsche Bahn AG, Disney Internet Guide, Dogpile, Encyclopaedia Britannica, Excite, FBI, GoTo.com, HotBot, Inference Find, Infoseek, Inktomi, Internet World, LookSmart, Lycos, Lycos SafetyNet, MetaCrawler, Metafind, NBC TV, Netscape Communications, NISS (National Information Services and Systems), Net Nanny, Net Shepherd, Northern Light, Search Engine Report, Search Engine Watch, Snap!, StreetMap created and hosted by BTex Ltd., SurfWatch, Tech Web, WebCrawler, WebTV Network, WhoWhere? Windweaver, Yahoo!, Yahooligans!, Yellow Pages, Yell: are registered trademarks or copyrights of their relevant organisations.

All other trademarks are the registered and legally protected trademarks of the companies who make the products. There is no intent to use the trademarks generically and readers should investigate ownership of a trademark before using it for any purpose.

I also acknowledge the following where Netscape pages are shown:

"Copyright 1998 Netscape Communications Corp. Used with permission. All Rights Reserved. This electronic file or page may not be reprinted or copied without the express written permission of Netscape".

"Netscape Communications Corporation has not authorized, sponsored, or endorsed, or approved this publication and is not responsible for its content. Netscape and the Netscape Communications Corporate Logos, are trademarks and trade names of Netscape Communications Corporation. All other product names and/or logos are trademarks of their respective owners."

Similar acknowledgements apply to all other screen shots, in particular from Excite:

"Excite and the Excite logo are trademarks of Excite, Inc. and may be registered in various jurisdictions. Excite screen display copyright 1995-1998 Excite, Inc."

Contents

5: Channels - Web Guides

6: Newsgroups

7: Recent & Helpful Specialist tools

8: Advanced Searching

1: Finding Information : An Introduction

The Internet has brought about a new technological revolution. It is claimed to be a "cultural revolution", but that depends on one's own definition of *culture*. What is more pertinent is that it is here to stay. Whether we like it or not, we shall be using the Internet and the WWW more and more to find information and to communicate with others.

The telephone, radio, TV, pocket calculators, fax machines, computers and e-mail are examples of technologies which few of us can seldom avoid using. Likewise, the WWW is fast becoming a technology which we shall have to become accustomed to using. Experience is beginning to suggest that certain kinds of information can be found more effectively via the Web than from more traditional printed sources.

Increasingly, some organisations are converting their information for display on the WWW. The Encyclopaedia Britannica, Which?, Yellow Pages and Job Centres are such examples.

What Kind of Information do people search for?
- the weather in a country we may be visiting tomorrow
- a reproduction of Jan Vermeer's painting, *"Girl with a Pearl"*
- jobs in the UK
- an e-mail address
- car sales, what is my car worth?
- research into plant or insect species
- Italian restaurants or plumbers in Rickmansworth
- a print out of a street plan of my own locality
- the meaning of a computing term - 'cookie' or 'ISDN'
- information about organisations (RSPCA, BPS)
- lists of Electronic Journals
- disqualified directors from Companies House
- stocks and share prices

1

- support groups for those with verbal dyspraxia
- times of trains from London to Aberdeen or Paris (and making bookings on-line!)

I could find any of these from a variety of sources; newspapers, books, magazines, journals, etc. But if I am connected to the Internet why not try that out? Not just for the UK but world wide.

How do I find that piece of information?

"Searching the Web has become as easy as clicking on a search button and entering a few keywords. In a few seconds you have your answer" ... or do we?

If we have been given the URL address of where the information is held, it can be typed into our browser's *location box*. But if we do not have a URL, then we have to search for the information. Many of us use our browser's search button to do this. The browser will then provide access to several search engines. But which one should we choose, is one better than another? Should we be using a search engine, a Web guide or Usenet [1]? How should the keywords for the subject we are looking for be constructed? The purpose of this text is to help us make these decisions in an informed manner.

As the Web grows, the need to search for and retrieve information must grow too. Typical users searching for uncomplicated topics have no trouble, except the sheer volume of results. Users requiring more complicated topics may increasingly have to rely on professional searchers, much as they do for online commercial databases. Such people will be skilled in search techniques. However, the purpose of this text is to help you find what you want by knowing about the various search techniques and tools available at the current time.

---

[1] Usenet pre-dates the Internet. It is a users' network where discussions take place on thousands of different topics. See Chapter 6.

So, how do we find information? There is no simple answer. There is no quick solution. At the time of writing, finding information on the Web is a skill. Like most skills, the more you practise the better you become. If you want to learn how to search effectively for information on the Web, then a little time, effort and practice is required. Having some basic understanding of how search engines work will enable you to make a more intelligent guess at the 'best' search engine to use and improve your chances of success.

Searching is becoming easier, not least because of commercialism. Those who put pages of information on the Web want them to be found. Web masters want their sites to be included in the listings. Search engines want us to use their product to increase their ratings and, hence, their advertising revenue. Consequently, their designers are improving and simplifying techniques for finding information. More intelligent search engine programs are being developed. We shall look at one later called: *AskJeeves*™

We also need to remember that the Web is not that old, in its present state, only since 1994. Yet in that time much has happened and much more is currently being developed. For example, many search engines can recognise only English words. But some are now beginning to expand their language repertoire.

For the present, we have to use the tools which are currently available. With these existing tools we should not approach them with the attitude:

> *"How do I find that piece of information?"*

but rather with the following attitude of mind:

> *"With the various tools available, what is my best chance of trying to find that piece of information?"*

How we go about it

In order to search effectively for information, we need to know a little about how search engines work, the range of search facilities available, how to reduce thousands of hits to a manageable number using advanced search techniques and some time and effort on our part. This text helps you with the first three but only you can do the fourth.

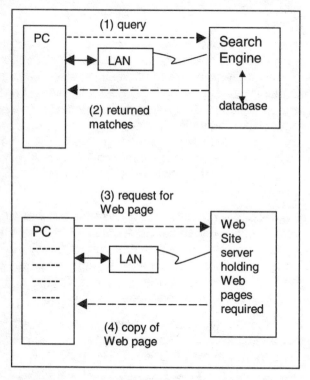

Four Stages in searching:

(1) request from office PC via LAN to search engine.
(2) search engine returns a list of matches.
(3) PC user selects a match from the list and a request for a copy of the Web page goes off to that site's server.
(4) Web server returns a copy of the Web page.

Chapter Summary:

Researchers, office workers, professionals, school children and other members of society are gradually becoming more dependent on the World Wide Web in order to find information. Currently it is an art form which requires a little knowledge and practice in order to conduct searches on the Web successfully. It is not as simple as clicking a few buttons, unless you want to be overwhelmed by thousands, even millions, of Web pages.

In this text, we shall cover all the necessary technical knowledge required, explain the types of searching facilities available and provide examples of how to construct keyword queries so that you can find what you need. That is provided the information is on the Web in the first place.

Certain types of information are not yet on the Web. For instance, if you wanted to research in depth the social history of the Tudors, study A-level Maths or learn about an obsolete musical instrument, you would be better off going to a reference library. Within ten years, such information will be more widely available on the Web as more educational material comes on-line.

Terms used:

browser	an application program, such as Netscape or Internet Explorer, which enables you to search the WWW for information and display it on your PC
keyword queries	words and phrases typed in by users when they want to find information
LAN	Local Area Network, frequently connected to the Internet
location box	a box provided by browsers into which a URL can be typed. See Appendix A
search button	a browser's icon button which when clicked displays a search page enabling users to type in their search queries
search engines	in this chapter, a general term, though not accurate, for any search facility used to find information

URL	Uniform Resource Locator: it provides the language used (a protocol such as http), the web site address and the document name of the page to be displayed
Usenet	discussion groups on the Internet frequently called Newsgroups
Web master	person responsible for maintaining web pages at a given site
WWW	World Wide Web

What is next?

We next look at the two main types of search engines and see how they work. This will enable us to make a choice between the two. They are *search engines* and *directories*. Subsequent chapters will unveil other types of search engines, some of which may be more appropriate than others for finding the sort of information we want. Being able to choose the right one may make the difference between finding what we want and not finding it.

In this chapter we cover some of the basic technical knowledge about search engines and how they work. It is an essential starting point for anyone who is serious about searching the Web. It will enable us to differentiate between the various search engines (and there are hundreds of them!) so that we can make an informed decision about which one is most appropriate at any given time.

Search Engines

If an organisation's web page is on a server which is connected to the Internet, then anyone can visit and read that page and make a mental or written note about its contents. If this page has links to other pages, then those links can be followed and their contents 'memorised'.

There are many companies which make a living out of doing precisely that. They have a list of sites and visit all of them on a regular basis to see what they have to offer, what is new and what has been changed since their last visit.

Details of what is found and where it was found is kept in a huge *index* or database. These indexes are owned and maintained by the individual search companies. When someone uses their search engine to find information, the keywords are matched against their own index and a list of web pages and their addresses is returned to the user.

How do they get the Lists?

Search engines are owned by organisations which have procured a list of major and minor site addresses and they regularly visit each of the sites on their list. These lists can be obtained in many ways. InterNIC (Internet Network Information Center) is an organisation which handles Internet domain name registration. Each new site has to register its site address for approval. In the UK, this can be done through various companies. Many Web masters also 'announce' their sites to the major search tools in the hope that these search providers will visit their sites and include their pages in their database. In other words, lists of sites can be obtained from a variety of sources, just like ordinary mailing lists.

How do they create the Indexed Database?
There are basically two methods by which the search companies collect the information held in their databases. One method is to send out *computer programs* to do all the hard work of visiting sites and returning with what they have found. These programs are what are the true search engines and are frequently referred to as *crawlers* or *spiders* or *robots* or just *bots*. AltaVista, Excite and Northern Light are three such excellent examples.

The other method uses *people*. They use their browsers, just as we do. They visit site addresses, look at the home pages and list all the material they find. They will also follow links to other pages mentioned. The proper term for this method is a *directory listing* or simply *directory*. Yahoo! and LookSmart are two examples. (See *A Modern Fairy Tale* on page 9.)

Frequently, both methods are inaccurately called *search engines*. But as you will see, it is often necessary to make an accurate distinction between search engines and directories especially when choosing a search tool. In these notes, *search tools* refer to any type of search facility; the companies which maintain them, are referred to as *search providers*. When it becomes necessary, we make a distinction between search engines and directories.

The main categories of Search Tools
There are five main categories of search tools:

- search engines
- directories, also called *hierarchies* or *subject trees*

- meta-search engines
- Web guides or channels for general topics, e.g.:
    entertainment, cars, travel, people, businesses,
    Usenet groups, health, finance, news items, etc.
- specialised search tools for specific topics, e.g.:
    Deja News - where you can find information about
    discussion groups
    TechWeb - for finding definitions of computer
    terms
    Deutsche Bahn AG - for train time-tables and
    more
    StreetMap - for street maps of the UK

A list of these and many others and where they can be
found is given in Chapters 7 & 10.

In this section, we shall restrict our discussion to search
engines and directories since the others are variations on
them. The other types of search tools will be introduced in
later chapters.

A Modern Fairy Tale

Yahoo! was one of the first search tools on
the Web. It is said that when two young
men went to study at an American
university, they spent much of their time
searching the Web and compiled a list of
their favourite sites. To their surprise, other
students found their list of great interest too.

They 'dropped out' of university and
decided to market the list and soon became
millionaires.

How Search Engines & Directories Work

Who Needs to Know & Why do we need to Know?
With some understanding of how search tools work you
can greatly improve your technique for finding information
and it will also provide you with the reasons why some

tools give you thousands of *hits* whilst others give you fewer; why you have never been able to find what you want; why you get duplicates; and, why the page you wanted is always the last in a list of 16,000.

Web authors also need to know how they work so that they may place appropriate keywords in the HTML code looked at by search engines.

Web masters require a much more detailed knowledge of the various search tools in order to increase the popularity of their own sites. (See Chapter 11 for some tips.)

Search Engines v. Directories
The information stored in the indexes is dependent upon an underlying technology. The more you appreciate that technology, the more you can harness it to your advantage.

Search Engines: A true search engine is a computer program which visits a web site and looks at the home page. It follows links from the home page to other pages. This implies that if other web pages are not mentioned on a home page, then they may not be 'found' by a search engine. Some search engines sample a web site and stop following links after a certain level. Some dutifully follow each link regardless of the depth it might lie down.

Some make a list of each word, whereas others will select certain words based on some pre-determined algorithm. The search engine returns all the links and keywords it has found and these are stored in a huge *index*. Search keywords entered by users are then matched against this index.

When we visit a web site via our browser, we are in fact behaving like a search engine. We do it manually, whereas search engines are programs designed to visit sites automatically and return lists of what they have found.

Directories: Yahoo! is a prime example of a pure *directory*. Web masters may submit a short description of what their entire site contains to a directory. Human beings look at the submission and if the material is suitable it will be added to their directory's index. Yahoo! employs some 80 people for this work.

In some cases, human editors employed by directory providers visit sites and compile a short description of whatever they think is of value.

The material is collated and compiled into categories and sub-categories. For example, there may be a *travel* category and another on *blood pressure* and the categories could be sub-divided as follows:

Main category	Sub-categories
Travel:	UK
Europe	Italy
	France, etc.
USA	New York
	Disney World
	Grand canyon, etc.
Blood Pressure:	cardiology
	heart disease
	hypertension
	heart (physiology), etc.

Some people refer to these directories as *hierarchies* or *search trees* because of the structure of the index.

When a search phrase is entered by users, this is matched against the categories in their index and a list of sites and web pages is returned to the user.

There are also *hybrid search engines*. These are pure search engines which also have an associated directory, so that you get the best of both worlds.

Most of the major search engines have always had an associated directory to complement their raw search results. But being so labour intensive little emphasis was placed on that part. Recently, however, the emphasis is on directories. It is a constantly changing arena.

In these notes, the general term *service provider* or simply *provider* is used when referring to the companies which own and maintain indexes. When used, *search engines* refer to the strict meaning of the term; likewise for *directory*.

Which to Choose?

In general, search engines have a much larger number of web pages in their index than directories. (Figures are given in the next chapter.) Does that mean that a search engine is the automatic choice? Not really. Search engines are compiled by programs whereas directories are compiled by humans. A directory has fewer pages but each has been carefully looked at by editors and put into categories. Consequently, returned matches via a directory, though fewer in number, may be far more relevant than thousands returned by a search engine.

For example, if the word *hotel* was used for a query, a search engine could return any page with the word "hotel" in it. A directory would look in a *hotel category*, present fewer matches but all highly relevant.

Here is an instance. One search engine gave over 500,000 hits for 'hotel' whereas a directory gave 703. The latter were all related to hotel guides, hotel reservations, even hotel jobs. Typing in *'hotels in UK'*, reduced this number to 50+. Typing the same phrase into the search engine actually increased the number to over a million. Why? Because of the addition of "UK". The search engine now gave Web pages offering luxury cruises from the UK and many other pages with UK in them.

Search Engines compared with Directories

From the above, it may seem that a directory would be a better tool to use, 500,000+ from a search engine against 50 odd from a directory. But there is more to it than simply numbers.

The example given is an unfair comparison between the two search tools. First of all, the word *hotel* was too vague for a search engine. However, by typing in "Hotels in UK" **and** using advanced features[1], the search engine returned 5060 hits. So now we have 50 as against 5060. Do we still go for the directory?

It will depend on what we really want. For example, if I wanted to conduct a survey on UK hotels, a search engine would be better. If I only want a short list of 3 - 5 star hotels in the UK, a directory would be more efficient.

However, a directory would probably not include many, if any, 2 or 1 star hotels or Bed and Breakfasts. After all, there is a limit as to how many sites human editors can review. Yet for students and backpackers, it would be these less expensive hotels which would be of more interest. Consequently, for them a search engine would be better than a directory since it can visit many more sites. So, it is not just a question of numbers.

Directories cannot look at all web sites because of the man-power involved. Search engines, on the other hand, send out their spiders which happily trawl many more Web sites and return with much more information.

It is early days in our tour of Web search tools and it may be that neither of the above would be the best tool to use. In Chapter 9, once all the tools have been discussed, we can really begin to make a much more informed guess at which tool should have been used.

---

[1] See Chapter 8 for how to use these advanced features.

How Search Engines are designed

A pure search engine has three main elements. First there is the *spider*, also called a *crawler* and *robot*. A spider visits a web site, reads the home page and follows any links to other pages within the site. The spider will return to the site on a regular basis, perhaps every few days or even a month or so, to look for changes.

What is found by a spider is entered into the second part of the search engine, the *index*. It may take some time for new pages found by spiders to be added to the index and until a page is indexed, it is not available to those using that search engine.

This index is a huge catalogue containing a copy of every Web page the spiders have found. If a web page changes, then the index has to be updated. Naturally, how 'fresh' or up-to-date an index is depends on how regularly spiders re-visit sites.

Search engine software is the third part of a search engine. This is the program which sifts through the millions of pages recorded in the index to match the search phrases entered by users. It then ranks the matches in an order which it thinks is relevant and based on the keywords used in the search query. When we type in a search phrase and click on a *search* button, it is this part which we use.

All search engines have these three parts. But each search provider will tune the parts in different ways. That is why different results are produced by each search engine even though the search phrase typed in is exactly the same. Some follow more links than others. Some visit sites more frequently. Some select all the words found, others select keywords found in certain parts of a page.

How Search Engines Rank Pages

We are not the only ones with a problem when faced with 20,000 odd matches in response to our keyword searches. Search tools have the same problem, namely, in which order to list the matches so that the most relevant do not appear at the bottom. Certain ranking strategies or algorithms are employed so that the "good" pages come at the top. New strategies are evolving all the time to improve ranking.

When a search is performed by a search engine, it searches through the millions of web pages stored in its index. The matches found will be ranked, so that the most relevant ones are listed first. Essentially, if you enter, say three keywords, all the pages containing those *three* keywords should come at the top of the list. Of course, search engines do not always succeed and some strange and non-relevant pages are listed. So you may have to do a little more digging, but by and large they do an amazing job. So what criteria are used?

Criteria used for Ranking

They follow a set of rules. One of the main rules involve the location and frequency of your keywords on a web page, sometimes referred to as the *location/frequency* method.

Location: A librarian would probably start searching for books on travel which had the word *'travel'* in the title. Search engines do the same and they look for your keywords in the titles of Web pages[2]. It assumes that pages with the keywords in their titles must be more relevant than those without.

Search engines will also check to see whether your keywords appear near the top of a web page, such as in headings or the first few paragraphs of text. They assume

---

[2] For web authors, this is the <TITLE> tag used in HTML.

that any page relevant to the search query keywords would mention those words early on.

Frequency is another main criterion. Search engines will analyse how often a keyword appears in relation to other words in the web page. Those which mention your keywords more frequently are deemed to be more relevant than a page with a lower frequency.

So far so good. All the major search engines follow these basic rules rather like all Italian cooks will add olive oil, garlic and parsley to certain recipes. But all good cooks have their own secrets about the quantity, quality and other little extras. That is what makes one cook different to another. So it is with search engines. Each one does something slightly different to the others. Thus, one search engine will produce a different set of hits and in a different ranking order to another. Hence our need to experiment and explore the various search engines until we find the one which suits us. Or, if our favourite occasionally fails to find what we want, we must try one of the others.

Boosts: Some search engines "boost" pages which match our search keywords. For example, WebCrawler uses link popularity as part of its ranking method. It can tell if a page in its index has many links pointing to it from the other pages in its index. It is assuming that if many pages point to a particular page, it must be 'good'.

Those search engines with associated directories may boost a page if it has been reviewed by one of the reviewers. The assumption is that if a page was good enough to be reviewed in the first place, it must be 'better' than one which has not been reviewed.

Some search engines, such as HotBot and InfoSeek, give a boost, if your search keywords appear in certain descriptive parts of a web page[3]. However, other search engines ignore these descriptive areas altogether.

Penalties: Some web authors try to improve their rank order by repeating keywords ad nauseam in their documents. This is known as *spamming* and some search engines will penalise, in some instances even ignore, those pages which have been 'spammed'. Hence, the best page may not even be listed!

Some search engines cannot follow links if these are in certain HTML features such as *frames* and *image maps* and hence pages which contain links to other pages via these features may never be 'crawled' and, therefore, may never be included in the index!

Returned Matches

Search tools will often provide a percentage value next to individual hits, such as 87%. This means how closely the document is ranked according to your query keywords. Many search engines tell you how many hits there are, but not all. Some search engines, such as Excite and AOL NetFind, include a '*More like This'* after some results. Were you to click on that phrase, that document would then be used as an example of what similar documents to look for. But it should be used with caution. Experiment a little first.

Sometimes, you will find references which have nothing to do with your original query. This is due to the fact that some search engines and directories will perform a concept or context based matching. For example, I was looking for information about the 'World Health Organisation'. So, those were the words I typed in as my search query. To my surprise I found a reference to 'Global Health' in the first five results listed. It had matched my word *'world'* to *'global'*.

---

[3] For web authors, these are the meta tags <META> in HTML.

It also gave a reference to "Arachnological Publications of the world", presumably because the word *'world'* appeared in that web page. (I did not know what it meant, either, apparently it is to do with *'cobwebs'*!)

You can begin to see the complexity of factors influencing how search engines rank and return information. It is your own experience, that means time spent comparing one with another, which will eventually influence which search tool suits you.

Although it seems incredible that a search engine can sift through millions of pages looking for your keywords in such a short time *(Yes, we sometimes have to wait, but the search at the other end only takes seconds.)*, searching and sorting techniques were one of the first computing activities to be programmed.

Mathematical techniques were applied and design methodologies implemented many decades ago. That is why computers are so fast at performing searches and matches. Just think how quickly a word processor can perform a spell check on a long document.

Chapter Summary:

We have made a distinction between search engines and directories and seen how search engines are designed.

At a simple level, some search engines index more pages than others. (See Table 3.2 on page 23.) Some will re-visit pages at a site more frequently than others, making their index more 'fresh' or up-to-date than others. Some search to a greater depth than others. Thus, no one search engine has exactly the same set of pages in its index to search through as another.

This is why one search tool finds something another cannot because of the depth of their searching.

Concept matching, whereby one word or phrase is associated with similar words, may also explain why a list of results contains the same document several times.

Since a directory is compiled by human beings, it may return fewer but more relevant matches than a search engine.

Returned matches are listed according to a strategy or set of criteria employed by the search tool. New ones are evolving all the time to improve returned lists so that the most relevant are listed first. To keep up-to-date with such advances, join the free *Search Engine Watch* e-mail report. The August 1998 report, number 21, discusses two new systems currently being used, *Direct Hit* and *Clever*. See page 89 for more information about *Search Engine Watch*.

Terms used:

concept matching	a feature used by some search tools to match original query words with others of a similar meaning, e.g. 'dog grooming' with 'pet care'
directory	a database of web pages and their contents created by human beings rather than computer programs
domain name	that part of a URL which specifies the address of a server, e.g. www.netscape.com identifies the address on the Internet of Netscape's server
hits	number of returned matches to a query
HTML	the languages used to create pages for the WWW
index	the vast database of sites and their contents used to find matches to keyword queries
link	a hypertext link which when clicked will display the Web page referenced by the link address

keywords	words entered by users to specify what they are looking for
ranking	techniques used by search providers to list hits in an order of relevancy
search engine	program which automatically crawls web sites
search providers	companies who provide access to their index
search tools	in this text, any search tool
server	in this text, a computer in a network of computers which is shared by multiple users. For example, a computer which maintains and stores all the Web documents at the site
spamming	in the context of search engines, entering the same word many times in the hope that the page may be put in a top list of matches
spider, robot, crawler	other terms for search engines

What is Next?

Now that we know something about how search tools work, which ones are the major players? There are hundreds and in the next chapter, we shall compare some of the popular search engines and directories so that we can decide which one to use or whether we would be better off using a meta-search engine.

3: Who's Who?

The Major Players

Having made a distinction between search engines and directories, we can look at some of the main search tools and begin to contrast them. This will allow us to make a choice of which type of search tool may be more convenient to use than another. New ones will come and older ones may disappear, but the following are the major search tools currently in use. We shall then look at meta-search engines in case we might be better off using one of them. Chapter 10 gives the home addresses of these main search tools.

The following table lists many of the major search tools, the year they began and whether they are a search engine or a directory.

Name	Year	Type
AltaVista	Dec 1995	Search Engine
AOL NetFind	Mar 1997	Search Engine
Excite	late 1995	Search Engine
HotBot	May 1996	Search Engine
InfoSeek	early 1995	Search Engine
LookSmart	Oct 1996	Directory
Lycos[1]	May 1994	Search Engine
MSN	mid-1998	Search Engine
Netscape Netcenter	June 1998	Search Engine
Northern Light	Aug 1997	Search Engine
Snap!	Sept 1997	Directory
WebCrawler	April 1994	Search Engine
Yahoo!	late 1994	Directory

Table: 3.1 Some popular search tools.

---

[1] The name Lycos comes from the Latin 'wolf spider'. I thought you might like to know that!

In Table 3.2, we summarise and contrast some of the major search engines according to the following criteria and for which statistics are available.[2]

Size: the number of Web pages they search through and hence the size of their index. Take the numbers with a grain of salt since some pages may be duplicated accidentally or appear in several database indexes. For this reason, search tools are usually categorised into big, medium and small. The numbers were correct at the time of writing.

Pages crawled per day: how many pages a search engine can index in a day. The more it can look for, the more likely it is to be up-to-date. However, some sites may well be visited more frequently than others, for example, if it is known that a site changes its pages more frequently than others. And see below under *freshness*.

Freshness: pages on the Web are constantly changing and it is not easy to maintain an index and keep it up-to-date. For example, a page which has been submitted may be indexed immediately. But it may take some time before the search engine visits the site to see whether any changes have been made to that page. More popular parts of the Web may be visited more often than other parts. Sites which advertise or pay for their pages to be listed by search engines will, naturally, get preferential treatment.

The table below, then, is a general guide but it should indicate the relative merits of the various search engines. Note that only search engines crawl the Web, hence there is no reference to directories. It will also explain why having found something in a listing, it may no longer be there when you click on the URL. It may have been

---

[2] Note: The statistics in this text were correct as of July 1998 and taken from a variety of sources. Some will have changed, even by the time you read this note. They are meant to be a general guide rather than rigidly factual.

deleted, moved to another folder or even had its contents changed since the index was last updated. Some indexes may be days old or even months old.

Name	Size in millions	Pages Crawled per day (millions)	Freshness
AltaVista	Big (140)	10	1 day - 1 month
Excite (AOL)	Big (55)	3	1-3 weeks
HotBot and MNS	Big (110)	10	1 day - 2 weeks
InfoSeek	Medium (30)	not available	minutes to 2 months
Lycos	Medium (30)	6-10	1-2 weeks
Northern Light	Big (30-50)	not available	2 weeks
WebCrawler	Small (2)	not available	weekly

Table: 3.2 Search Engines Compared

In the case of directories, these are maintained by humans who have to keep visiting sites. The freshness of their index may not be the same as search engines. In some cases, they may have to rely on being told by Web masters that pages have changed.

Affiliations & Partnerships with the Search Providers
In the following table, you will quickly realise that when using one search tool, your queries may well be forwarded to other search tools which are affiliated to the one you are using. This is all to the good!

Name	Partnered or affiliated in some way with:
AltaVista	LookSmart in 1998
AOL NetFind	basically Excite
Excite	acquired Magellan in July 96 and WebCrawler in Nov 96. Both still run as separate services. Serves AOL & Netscape
HotBot	added LookSmart 98 , powered by Inktomi *
InfoSeek	runs a Directory as well. Serves Cnet's Search.com

Name	Partnered or affiliated in some way with:
LookSmart	used by AltaVista & HotBot. LookSmart uses AltaVista when its own search fails
Lycos	has an associated directory called Web Guides. It also runs Top 5% - reviewer based listings
MSN	powered by Inktomi* (like HotBot). Yahoo! to be re-created within MSN
Netscape Netcenter	basically Excite
Northern Light	has a Special Collection[3] of 2000+ additional sources including: magazines, books, journals, databases and news wires.
Snap!	from CNet (The Computer Network). Queries not found are piped to Inktomi *
WebCrawler	purchased by AOL in Mar 95 and then by Excite in Nov 96. It runs as a separate service
Yahoo!	queries not found via Yahoo! are piped to Inktomi *

Table: 3.3 Affiliations between Search Tools
See page 41 for information about Inktomi.

Meta-search Engines
Meta-search engines, such as *Dogpile*, *Inference Find*, *MetaCrawler* and *Metafind* are sites to which you can submit a query. They do not own their own indexed databases. These sites forward your query to a number of popular search engines, directories and other specialised indexes. Results found are a compilation from a variety of these separate search tools.

Some display results from each search tool in sequence. Others sort the results and eliminate duplications which could arise if the same page occurs in different indexes. Some allow you to specify a sort order; with others it is based on significant words and phrases used in the

---

[3] There is a fee for using the Special Collection of $1 - $4 a time or a monthly fee. But see latest details at: http://www.nlsearch.com/   Northern Light offers a free web search in addition to the Special Collection.

search query. Try out several meta-search engines to find which one you prefer.

Some meta-search engines allow you to specify a time-period to wait for results, such as 20 or 40 seconds. The longer you are prepared to wait, the more results you will get.

Meta Search engines

Dogpile	Inference Find	MetaCrawler	Metafind
AltaVista	AltaVista	AltaVista	AltaVista
Excite Search	Excite Search	Excite	Excite
& Subject	InfoSeek	InfoSeek	HotBot
guide	Lycos	Lycos	InfoSeek
HotBot	WebCrawler	WebCrawler	OpenText
InfoSeek	Yahoo!	Yahoo!	WebCrawler
Lycos			
Lycos a2z			
Magellan			
PlanetSearch			
WWW Worm			
WWW Yellow			
Pages			
WebCrawler			
What-U-Seek			
Yahoo!			

Table 3.4 Meta-search Engines and which search tools they

Concept Matching
Some search tools will conduct a concept match on the keywords used. For example, World Health Organisation (WHO) was matched in one of my searches with pages on *Global Health. Elderly* could be matched with *Senior Citizens*, etc. Although the number of returned matches are greater, they may well prove to be of value to a serious researcher.

Excite uses an exclusive technology which it calls *ICE* (Intelligent Concept Extraction). It learns how new words and ideas are related to other words and ideas. One example it gives is that of "dog care" being matched with "pet grooming". It would find pages with *dog care* in them but also provide pages with *pet grooming*, even those these words were not entered by the user.

Another example is Ask Jeeves™ which uses sophisticated natural language processing to understand and match users' questions to its own extensive knowledge base.

A word such as *longest* may also be matched with words such as tallest, *widest*, *highest*, *fastest*, etc. So when I entered a query via Ask Jeeves to find *"the longest river in the world"*, I was given additional matches for the tallest Ferris wheel, the largest diamond, the fastest animal. These were politely put in a separate section entitled: *"You may also be interested in these questions."* Although I did not ask for this information, it proved to be of some personal use.

Search engines v. Directories v. Meta-search engines
Which one should we choose?

Meta-search engine
Choose a meta-search engine if you are relatively new to searching and have not yet decided on a favourite search engine. Meta-search engines are also useful to older hands when they want to get an overall feel for what is out there. The hits will be large but can be cut down to size by using the advanced search features. For example, a list of 1 million matches was reduced to a respectable 44 within a matter of seconds using advanced searching techniques. (See Chapter 8.) Meta-search engines can produce some very admirable results and are particularly useful for those researching topics.

Search Engines

Search engines are useful when you want a broad feel for your subject matter. But which one to choose? That is up to you. You will need to search for the same subject with the same keywords using a variety of search engines, compare their results and choose the one which suits you. Bear in mind that because of partnerships and affiliations one search engine may automatically pass your queries on to another. So read the tables above carefully to avoid duplicating your effort. For example, if you choose Excite, do not then choose Netscape's Netcenter or AOL's NetFind since both are powered by Excite.

Having said this, Netscape and NetFind will tweak the results sent back by Excite. You may prefer one of their presentations to Excite's presentation, or vice versa. Also, as we shall discuss in later chapters, each provider will offer its own range of additional services and even allow you to personalise (see page 94) their search page. One set of offerings may suit you more than another. So, back to the caution in the Preface. The more you compare the various search engines, the better you will be able to decide which suits your particular taste.

Directories

Because directories are compiled by human beings and not by programmed spiders, the number of pages which they hold in their databases (indexes) are much smaller than those generated by search engines. Your resulting matches are therefore going to be fewer. But, whereas search engines have to look through web documents to find matches based on your keywords, directories tend to look in their carefully compiled categories to match your keywords. Hence, the results may frequently be fewer but more relevant.

The recent growth of Snap! and LookSmart is good news for those who like directories. We now have a choice of directories. Previously, Yahoo! was the only major directory and seldom figured in comparisons with true search engines. It will have to keep up its good performance in the face of competition.

Conclusions

Directories should be chosen when the subject matter is likely to fall into a common category and when you do not want too many results. Choose a search engine if you want a broad and comprehensive feel for what is on the Web and especially if the subject matter is a bit esoteric. You will need to use advanced search features in order to refine the quantity of matches.

If you are not sure where to begin or if you need to conduct some serious research, try one of the meta-search engines. They search all the big databases, return a huge list of matches but, you ought to find something of value to use as a starting point.

Most Web searchers eventually discover their own favourite search engine. If that fails to produce what they want, then they try some of the others. My own favourite search engine is Northern Light (see Chapter 10 for the home page). The main reason is that it not only has a large index comparable in size to AltaVista and Inktomi, but the returned matches are put into categories such that it becomes easy to select the most appropriate for the subject in hand. An example is discussed on page 80. If you are new to searching, try it out and compare the same query results from one of the other large search engines. In the end, it all boils down to a matter of personal taste.

Chapter Summary:

There are a number of major search engines, directories and meta search engines. Entering a query with one will invariably mean that your query will also be passed to one or more of the other players. If you have a favourite search tool, it is in your own interest to find out which other search tools it has affiliations with so that you will not conduct a separate and wasted search using one which has already been used.

Meta-search engines are a good place to start since they forward your query to many more search providers. Search engines and meta-search engines are usually a better starting point if you have an unusual or esoteric subject to hunt down.

Still confused? It may take a while to sort out all the affiliations and partnerships. In Chapter 9, we shall draw all the threads together. For the moment, we are simply trying to provide an overview of what tools are available. Then, we shall be in a position to make an informed judgement about which search tool to use. In any case, there are many specialised search tools now appearing in an abundance. These are discussed in Chapter 7 and may well prove to be more appropriate for certain searches than the standard search tools so far mentioned.

Finally, what you see today may not look the same tomorrow. Search providers change things, such as their display pages or their keyword search algorithm; some become eaten up by others, new ones appear and old ones go! Therefore, you need to keep up to date with the changing scene. In Chapter 10, there is a reference to one site that keeps you up to date and for free, *Search Engine Watch*.

Terms Used:

concept matching	a technique whereby words entered in a search query are matched in context with other similar words. For, example, elderly could be matched with senior citizen, OAP, etc.
ICE	Intelligent Concept Extraction, used by Excite

Meta-search engines	queries are sent to several search tools

What is Next?
We have looked at some of the major players, but where do we find them? That is the subject of the next chapter.

Some Things to Try
Try the following to get some feel for the different types of search tools.

1. Use a search engine, such as InfoSeek, and enter 'hotels' as your query. Note the number of hits. Then use a directory, such as Yahoo! or LookSmart, and enter the same query. Compare the results. (You will find the search pages to these search tools in Chapter 10.)

2. Now try a meta-search engine, such as Dogpile, with the same query. Compare the results with the above. Try to work out how results are returned by the meta-search engine. Are the various results in a list or by search tool used or how? If you used Dogpile, you should find that the results from each search tool used is listed in turn. This is a useful way of getting a feel for a variety of tools without using each one separately.

3. For all the tools you chose, look for an *About LookSmart* (or whatever) link and read up about the search tool.

4. Using the same queries, compare the results from Northern Light with some of the other search engines.

4: Portals: Gateways to the Web

In Chapter 3, we mentioned a number of the popular search tools. In this chapter we look at what Netscape, Internet Explorer, and ISPs, such as AOL and CompuServe offer and why. You can then decide for yourself whether you are content with their choice or whether you wish to explore and use some of the other search tools not displayed on their search pages.

It is said that about 50% of Web searchers use their browser's *search button* to find information on the Web. The other 50% are the more discerning Web searchers who will have *bookmarked* their own favourite search tools. Chapter 10 provides the home page addresses for many of the other popular tools not shown by the main browsers or ISPs.

When I first began, I, too, used the browser's search button. I was a given a choice of about five search engines and thought that they were the only ones I could use. It was not until later that I realised that there were in fact hundreds, some of which were far better suited to my needs than those displayed by my browser.

In the following, some history is included and may be skipped unless you would like to understand more of the background alliances between the major browsers, ISPs and the major search tools.

Portals

The search pages of AOL, CompuServe, Netscape and Internet Explorer and many of the major search engines such as Excite, AltaVista, InfoSeek, etc., are known as *portals*, that is they are gateways to the Web. Not only do they offer a straightforward search facility via their own search engine and/or directory, but they also provide other services which we shall look at in the next chapter.

Essentially, these portals want us to keep returning to their search pages by providing a whole range of services which they think will appeal to us. Why? Because the more people who visit their sites, so-called *traffic*, the more revenue they can ask for from those who advertise with them.

This is why so many[1] search pages are cluttered with animated advertising banners, logos and other prominently placed links to their sponsors.

It is rather like magazines, each vying for our "support" by offering a range of services, over and above a pure search facility, by which means they hope to be able to keep us coming back to their portal. Another wheeze used is to allow us to personalise (*'personalize'* in English American spelling) their search pages. See page 94 for an example from Excite.

As you will find out from the following history sections, the main browsers change their search pages from time to time as well as the list of search providers. Experienced web searchers are aware of this and are able to adjust accordingly.

Netscape:
When pressing the *Net Search* button or by defaulting to the Netscape home page, Netscape loads its own search page listing six of the major search providers. Thousands of people visit this Net Search page every day.

In June 1998, Netscape changed its search page (to the one shown on page 33) and is now running its own branded search engine, *Net Search*. It is powered by Excite, in the same way that AOL's own AOL NetFind is powered by Excite. 25% of the time, Netscape will display its own *Net Search* when the search button is pressed. Another 25% of the time is given to Excite. The remaining

---

[1] See GoTo.com at http://www.goto.com/ which deliberately sets out to remove all the 'clutter'. Look in the *About GoTo* for more information.

50% of the time is rotated amongst Infoseek, Lycos, AltaVista and LookSmart, but they do not say how much time is allocated to these others. By 1999, Netscape will display its own search page 50% of the time with Excite still at 25%. If you keep clicking on the *Net Search* button, you will see that the search providers keep rotating. If you were really keen, you could work out the percentages for each one.

Why these providers? Because they pay millions of dollars for the privilege. These are called the *premier* providers. Note that LookSmart is the one chosen in the illustration below. But by clicking on one of the other search engines, that provider's form would appear in place of LookSmart.

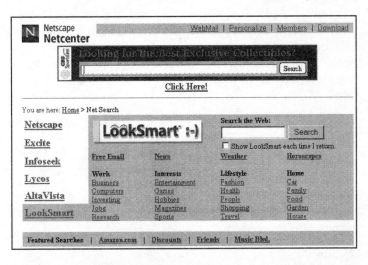

In addition to the main search box, lists of other services are displayed, the subject of the next chapter. In the above illustration, LookSmart has them displayed under four main headings: *Work, Interests, Lifestyle* and *Home*. Page 43 shows the *search form* from Netscape and has a similar set of services but displays them in an alphabetical order. Some are the same as LookSmart but have a different wording, for example, *Autos* instead of *Car*.

Note also that under the search box is another box saying: "*Show LookSmart each time I return.*" which if selected will keep returning to that search engine each time you call up Netscape's search page. All the others have this same box with their name next to it.

The Netscape *Search* button, irrespective of which search engine is displayed, provides lists of additional Web service providers under various categories, see page 45. This is covered in more detail in the next chapter. These are called *marquee* providers. They too have to pay for this privilege but less than premier providers because they are not displayed so prominently.

Netscape History
Originally, Yahoo! was the main service provider to be listed by Netscape. With the launch of Excite in late 1995, this became the preferred service link. Changes took place again in April 1996. Search engines and directories were paying $5 million to have a premier spot on this page.

In May 1997, the page changed yet again to display four premier providers. This time, no one was saying how much was being paid. It was tied in to the amount of traffic each provider received from Netscape's search page.

Five marquee providers, LookSmart, Snap!, WebCrawler, AOL NetFind and HotBot were listed but less prominently than the premier ones.

Microsoft:
Microsoft has its own search page which is displayed when you click the *Search* button. Internet Explorer also lists premier search providers. These are accessed and displayed differently depending on which version of Internet Explorer you have. However, Microsoft is about to change its search page to reflect its own MNS. What is shown below was current in June, 1998.

Internet Explorer 3: displays six premier providers rotating equally amongst them. These are InfoSeek, Yahoo!, Magellan, Excite, AltaVista and Lycos.

Internet Explorer 4: tends towards frames. In one frame (or pane) a premier list is displayed with Yahoo! pre-selected. It has a slight edge. The second pane displays the page selected from the first frame. See page 36 for an example. What we see below is the current (June 1998) list of premier providers displayed by Internet Explorer 4.

Microsoft's search page is continually being restructured. At the time of writing (June, 1998), Microsoft is set to launch its own search engine. It is called MSN at the moment. Yukon was the project's 'working' name, but no formal name has yet been selected at the time of this writing.

Microsoft is said to be partnering with Inktomi to add a search feature to its own existing web site. Exactly how the search feature will be integrated is still being planned at the time of my writing, but it is said that it will be prominent. In addition to its own search engine, Microsoft is said to be working with Yahoo! to enhance its own directory. Existing MSN directory listings will be added, but Yahoo!'s own listings will make up the bulk of the directory.

Microsoft History

Yahoo! used to be the default selection but the page changed in 1996 and again in 1997 to show other search providers. Since then, some providers have been dropped or taken over by other providers.

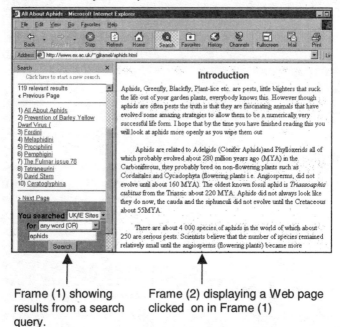

Frame (1) showing results from a search query.

Frame (2) displaying a Web page clicked on in Frame (1)

Figure 4.1: How IE4 uses frames for search results.

Tip: Clicking the *Search* button on Microsoft's IE4 toolbar will fill the screen with the second frame. Clicking the *Search* button again displays both frames.

Internet Service Providers (ISPs)

Service providers, such as WebTV, AOL and CompuServe, have a large number of followers. Where are they directed?

AOL: AOL directs its 8+million users towards an AOL-branded version of Excite called AOL NetFind. It draws from the Excite database but has its own look and feel about it.

WebCrawler was AOL's default search engine until the summer of 1996, Excite being the second choice. Excite purchased WebCrawler in November 1996. You may begin to see how interwoven the various providers are. Of course, it will keep changing and probably has done so since these notes were written.

CompuServe: CompuServe sends its 3+ million users to its Internet search page. One of four search engines is chosen randomly if the CompuServe search button is used. Lycos was the default search engine in 1997 but, in early 1998, it was alternated with AltaVista, InfoSeek and LookSmart.

WebTV:

> ".. *approximately 250,000 subscribers have joined the WebTV Network™. A key element of the company's success has been its unique method of delivering the Internet to consumers in a compelling format that matches the entertainment value they expect from TV.*"
> quoted from their page at:

`http://www.webtv.net/ns/about/backgrounder.html`

According to the press release[2], Excite has been the default search engine for users who select the search button from the WebTV home page since the partnership between the two companies began in October 1996.

We can expect similar alliances when TV set top boxes arrive in the UK for the mass consumer market.

On the Horizon
US media and communications giants are trying to gain control of the Internet portals. The NBC TV network announced in June 1998 that it was taking 60% of the Snap! web site.

---

[2] `http://corp.excite.com/press/081297webtv.html`

Walt Disney Co. have moved to acquire 43% of InfoSeek. Disney will use InfoSeek to host its media interests, the SportsZone and ABC TV channels.

AT&T, the telecommunications company made advances to AOL but were rejected.

We shall have to wait and see what all this will mean. The point is that we must not be surprised if our favourite search engine suddenly takes on a new and unexpected look and begins to charge for special quality searches. As Web searchers we need to be aware of what is going on behind the scenes. See *Search Engine Watch* where you can keep yourself up-to-date. (The address of the home page is in Chapter 10.)

What about the Meta-search Engines?
These seldom, if ever, appear either in the premier or the marquee positions. Thus, the canny searcher will bookmark a favourite for personal use.

TV Set Top Boxes

TV *set top boxes* are devices which can be attached to our TV sets and allow us access to the Web. It is already common in the USA and will be available in the UK in due course. Be warned! These devices are unlikely to offer the freedom of the Web currently enjoyed by PC users who have a choice of service providers. The set top box may limit our choice of search tools and services to whatever is provided. Think of it as going into a supermarket. You can choose only from whatever range of goods is offered by that supermarket.

Chapter Summary:
Which browser you use will affect which search providers are displayed. This is one reason why so many people, about 50% of users, bookmark their favourite search

provider rather than blindly use the Netscape or Microsoft Search button which will bring up that browser's own search page and search tools.

Does it matter whether AOL, Netscape's Net Search or Excite is used since they all use the Excite index? Not really! AOL and Netscape will tweak results according to some policy of their own and each will provide a different set of Web services. What will influence your choice may well depend on how one service provider displays and ranks results and what additional services it may offer. Again, you need to look at them all and compare and then make your informed decision.

Mergers, alliances and take-overs and all the razzmatazz associated with business practices mean that search tools are continually changing. Discerning Web searchers are aware of this and are not surprised by sudden changes in the look and feel of their search tools. Keep abreast of developments via *Search Engine Watch*.

When you wish to find information you have a choice. You can either use your browser's search button or use your favourite search tool. The latter can be selected from your bookmarks or, as many users seem to do, it can be selected to become the start page each time the browser is opened.

Terms Used:

bookmark	a page you wish to visit regularly can be bookmarked. The browser will note the URL address and make a note in its list of bookmarks. The bookmark can be clicked rather than the user having to type in the URL each time
frame	where a web screen is divided into two or more sections or separate windows. Typically, clicking on a link in one frame, will display the contents in another without the first being altered

ISP	Internet Service Provider
marquee	sites listed by portals in prominent positions on their Web pages in order to advertise them but not so prominently as premier clients
portals	a term used to describe a provider who offers more than just simple searching on the Web. They include access to special databases devoted to specific topics, such as travel, jobs, entertainment, buying and selling cars
premier	sites listed by portals in highly prominent positions on their Web pages in order to advertise them
search page	a web page which allows users to find information by entering queries into a search box. Because the service is free, these search pages are cluttered up with adverts for other companies and products
TV set top boxes	devices which can be attached to TV sets and provide a link to the WWW

What is next?

So far we have concentrated on search engines, meta-search engines and directories. It is now time to look at some other tools so that we can decide whether we should be using them for some of our searches. The next chapter discusses Web Guides.

Some Things to Try

1. Make a note of the search tools your browser offers.

2. Check the version number of your browser if you do not know what it is. To do so, click on the *About* option in the *Help* menu.

3. If you are using Netscape, keep clicking the *Net Search* button to cycle through the various premier providers. Look at the search form for each provider and see what the differences are and how they display their additional services.

Inktomi

Inktomi is the company which powers HotBot and several other search engines world-wide. As of June 1998, Snap!, Yahoo! and Microsoft picked Inktomi as their preferred service to automatically forward queries to when their own indexes fail to find any matches.

Inktomi does the crawling and maintains a central index. The other services tap into this source but the results produced by each one are tweaked in some way to make their results look different to the others.

Therefore, will there be any difference between using HotBot, Snap! and MSN? Probably not. Their search pages will look different, of course, and the results will be customised to look different. Custom crawling may also produce slightly different results. But essentially, they will remain close cousins.

Inktomi is the brains behind many other search services, such as GoTo.com, but does not compete with them as a service in its own right. It does the work but allows its partners to select and rank results according to their own algorithms.

It is suggested that the Inktomi database may become segmented in due course. For example, one segment may contain pages from only high quality Web sites, for which a fee may be levied.

The Internet is quite capable of collecting small sums of monies which would not be cost effective using traditional invoicing systems.

Do you need Digital Images?

There are a number of research programmes exploring the use and management of digital images. Some require a fee, others are free. Check the addresses below for specific details of cost and what is currently available.

Note how this illustrates the gradual building up of educational material on the Web. Within ten years or so, much more will have been added and made available to researchers.

MIDRIB: Medical Images Digitised Reference Information Bank, a project undertaken by staff at St. George's Hospital Medical School in collaboration with the Wellcome trust. Its aim is to create, maintain and deliver a comprehensive collection of medical images in digital form, for use in teaching and research.

http://www.midrib.ac.uk/

BAMBI: Better Access to Manuscripts and Browsing of Images provides a means of accessing ancient manuscripts. Microfilm is being converted into electronic form to ensure that ancient manuscripts are permanently recorded and available.

http://www.ilc.pi.cnr.it/bambi.html

SCRAN: a Millennium project to build a networked multimedia resource base for the study, teaching and appreciation of history and material culture in Scotland.

http://www.scran.ac.uk/

British Library's Digital Library Programme has absorbed the Initiatives for Access activities. These include the Treasures Digitisation Programme intending to widen access to irreplaceable treasures by digitising them and making them available over the networks.

http://portico.bl.uk/

Telematics for Libraries: The EU Telematics programme has funded a number of imaging projects, mostly targeted on library applications of the technologies. It can provide useful background and technical information.

http://www2.echo.lu/libraries/en/projects.html

5: Channels - Web Guides

We have covered search engines and directories and seen that meta-search engines submit queries to a range of tools. What we shall now look at are some of the other services frequently offered by the major portals, since these may well prove more appropriate ways of finding certain types of information, for example, jobs, travel, people, addresses, buying and selling cars.

These are the so-called Web Guides, Channels or Webliographies (not my word!) and all have a similar meaning. They are additional search tools but are limited to searching for information under certain topics.

The above shows part of the Netscape search page, as it appears when displayed on our screens. The scroll bars (not shown) are used to display more of the screen, see page 45. The Netscape search page[1] is obtained by clicking the *Net Search* button, unless you have chosen it to be the default start up page.

Note how the *search box* into which you type your search query is prominent on the top right (below *Search the Web:*) and the fact that it is powered by Excite also appears prominently at the bottom left. It also displays its *premier* search providers at the left hand side.

---

[1]   At the time of writing, Internet Explorer has not revealed its own search page.

The rest of the screen is taken up by a list of services under various categories: *Autos*, *Business*, *Computing*, *Education*, etc., in alphabetical order. Selecting one of the premier providers will display that search tool's list of Web guides as well as access to its search box.

See page 46 for AltaVista's Web services and page 33 for LookSmart's services. They differ slightly and one set may suit your taste more than another, as with magazines. In the case of AltaVista, it also offers different languages. We can expect to see an increase in different languages from many of the other service providers over the next year. For example, Yahoo! is currently working on a Spanish edition and has a dual language on some of its pages.

By choosing one of the categories you have access to a variety of information and services, much more than is mentioned in the following:

Autos, for example, provides information about:

- selling and buying cars, on-line if you wish
- owners' manuals for car maintenance, complete with diagrams
- insurance polices and financial quotes (of course!)

Sports covers the major activities: baseball, soccer, tennis, golf, etc. Very useful during the World Cup and Wimbledon. Order of play, information about the contestants, statistics, and so on are provided. (Sport fans should also see the next Chapter about how to join discussion groups. For example, during the World Cup fever - Wimbledon or any other sport - one could read and join in discussion groups about how England fared during the series; how one or other players 'lost' the series for us, the best goal scored, etc. It is a bit like going to a local pub and hearing what people think about certain issues, except that on the Web, the 'pub' is expanded nation and world wide.)

News covers the major headline news under various topics. It also includes world newspapers as a separate option: an impressive list, e.g. Asahi Newspaper, Tokyo; The Australian Online; Bangkok Post; The Irish Times, The Times, London; India Abroad; NeWo: News Resource for news and weather around the world.

Below this section are references to other major search tools, called *marquee* or sometimes *distinguished partners*. HotBot, WebCrawler and GoTo.com are under the heading: *Search the Web* (meaning search engines).

Snap!, Yahoo!, the Electric Library Research, etc., are under the *Explore by Topic* heading (meaning directories). Selecting one of these will go to that provider's search page. Whereas, selecting one of the premier search tools will allow access to that tool's search facility and Web guides, but the Netscape search page will remain the same. Try it out. If you do not want to use Netcenter, bookmark your own favourite search tools' home pages.

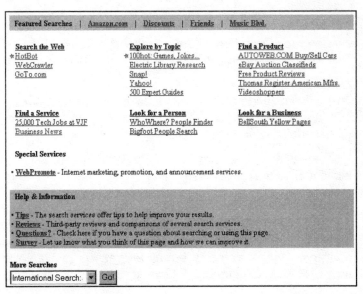

At the bottom is an important button which many search providers include. It allows users to select which country they wish to search in. For example, Australia, Sweden, Japan, UK, Italy, etc. Clearly, this is necessary for someone searching for jobs, travel, buying or selling cars, and so on within their own country.

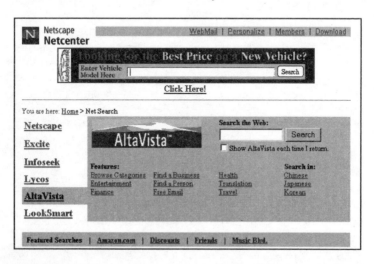

Looking for Cars, News items, Travel discounts, Jobs?
Use a Web guide and select your own country.

Looking for People?
Use a Web guide and select *'Find a Person'* (AltaVista), *'Bigfoot People Search'* or *'WhoWhere? - People Finder'* (Netscape's Netcenter), *'White Pages'* (Snap!).

Certain Web sites provide searchable databases of individual e-mail addresses and other "people-finding" tools. They may include residential telephone numbers and street addresses. However, unlike phone company white pages, there is no single source for this information, and you may have to try several sources. There is no guarantee that a person's e-mail address is available in any of these directories. Below is the result of using

46

LookSmart's *People* category. Note the cascading lists opposite the little arrows - ▶

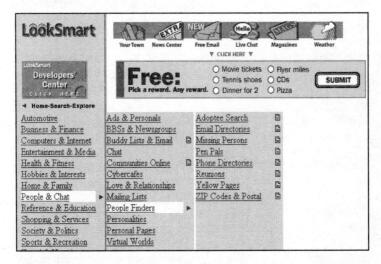

WhoWhere? is one source that I found very simple to use and reasonably effective.

Looking for a business?

Use a Web guide's *yellow pages* such as BellSouth from Netcenter or Yell from Internet Explorer. The latter offers a UK page. These Web sites provide searchable databases of business listings. Some also include additional information such as maps, driving directions, and Web addresses.

Some search tools, HotBot for example, will allow access to Usenet newsgroups. This is yet another way of finding information or, to be more accurate, of finding what others are saying about a particular topic. This is discussed in the next Chapter.

Chapter Summary:

Each provider has its own layout and set of categories, although, most have a basic set of categories. It is a little like magazines or newspapers all of which have certain features or topics in common. But each has a slightly different slant and maybe the odd feature which others do not have.

Terms Used:

marquee	sites listed by portals in prominent positions on their Web pages in order to advertise them but not so prominently as premier clients
premier	sites listed by portals in highly prominent positions on their Web pages in order to advertise them
search box	the box provided by browsers and search tools into which you type your query keywords
Web Guides	also called *channels*. Indexed web pages related to specific topics, e.g. autos, finance, games, health, travel
white pages	directories containing names and addresses of people
yellow pages	directories containing names and addresses of businesses

What is Next?
There are also discussion groups on a whole variety of subjects. Some can be a complete waste of time, but for some groups, the discussions can be of value. It is a simple matter to find and join in such groups.

Some Things to Try
1. Pick a topic from one of the service providers, say cars, and compare it with the same service offered by some of the other providers.

2. See whether you can find your e-mail address by using one of the 'People Finder' services.

6: Newsgroups

Newsgroups:

Yet another means of finding information is by reading the posted messages of discussion groups and, perhaps, even joining in. These are sometimes referred to as *Usenet groups* or *Newsgroups* or *BBS* (Bulletin Board Systems). Suppose you have a particular interest in a health problem such as *rheumatoid arthritis*. It is possible that people have been discussing this already and you can follow the *threads* of this discussion. A thread is where someone begins a discussion and another person replies, and yet someone else replies to that. These are the so-called *threads*. Some are painfully banal, but others may well be of interest.

You can follow a discussion from Netscape's *Window* menu by selecting *Netscape News* (in version 3 but version 4 has a special button). How you do so from Internet Explorer will depend on which version you are using. However, there are many newsgroup programs available which are very easy to use? An excellent one is DejaNews® (see page 50).

There are about 25,000+ discussion groups. Each one comes under a major topic such as *sci* for science and engineering, *rec* for recreational topics. Each of these is further subdivided into other categories, some into a thousand+. Here are a few, just to give a flavour. Many sub-groups are also sub-divided into further sub-groups.

USENET Group	Meaning	Sub-Groups	Sample sub-groups
alt	alternative	1765	activism; adoption; alcoholism; anagrams; archery; architecture; banjo; beer
comp	computing matters	869	AI; bugs; compilers; databases; fonts; multimedia; viruses

USENET Group	Meaning	Sub-Groups	Sample sub-groups
humanities	humanities	8	classics; sanskrit; shakespeare
ieee	Institute of Electrical and Electronics Engineers	12	general; pcnfs
misc	miscellaneous	127	creativity; education; entrepreneurs; handicapped; health
news	Usenet matters	29	announce.newusers; announce.conferences
rec	hobbies, games, recreational groups	658	animals.wildlife; birds; folk.dancing; heraldry
sci	science and engineering	188	agriculture; aeronautics; chem; fractals
soc	social issues	243	adoption; atheism; feminism; men; libraries; retirement
uk	UK matters	213	d-i-y; environment; people.deaf; people.rural; religion; jobs.offered

Deja News[1]

If a topic is discussed under several different categories, Deja News can prove very useful. For example, I typed in "12th century poetry" and found 10 matches but under several different sub-groups, such as:

```
alt.games.whitewolf; alt.books.cs-lewis;
alt.philosophy.debate.
```

It would have been a mammoth task to have manually searched all the sub-groups in the `alt` group to discover those ten matches. Yet, Deja News returned them within seconds.

---

[1] The home page is: `http://www.dejanews.com/`.

Typing in "rheumatoid arthritis" gave me 503 matches from groups such as `alt.support.arthritis` and `misc.health.arthritis`.

Some of these were more than just idle chatter. They proved to be serious discussions about this disease, its potential cures and relief as well as references to web page documents which discuss the matter at some length. Joining such a group, may well keep you up-to-date about this painful disease.

How to Subscribe to a Newsgroup
The word *subscribe* does not mean paying any money, it means *joining in for free*. There are various ways someone can subscribe to a newsgroup, either via:

`news:announce.newusers` which is the Usenet's "welcome page" for new users. You can type this into your browser's location box.

or, via the subscribe facility in one of the newsgroup programs. Deja News makes subscribing very easy. You first have to register with Deja News by clicking on *My Deja News* from any of its Web pages. This requires you to enter some details: name, gender, age, etc. Then click on the *Register Me!* button. Full details about how to subscribe are available on the registration page.

Deja News also makes it easy to *unsubscribe* to any of the discussion forums you may have joined. Yet another advantage (and I have no shares in the company) is that Deja News carries many more forums, over 50,000, than most ISPs can accommodate. It also has exclusive forums not found on any other site!

For Serious Research
Using a search engine, I arbitrarily chose Excite, I got over 400,000 hits for "rheumatoid arthritis". Many of these were serious papers on this subject. It also listed 44 recent news articles from a variety of medical journals.

Furthermore, I was also given sub-categories[2] by which I could narrow my search to a more specific area, for example: osteoarthritis, joints, gout spondylitis, rheumatic, rheumatology. Choosing osteoarthritis 'narrowed' the field to 43,625.

Having found material from the research papers listed by a search engine, a serious researcher may then wish to see whether that particular point is being discussed in Usenet and, if not, perhaps start a discussion.

Usenet Background
Usenet was the original discussion forum set up in 1979. Today it uses the Internet technology to transfer files between users' news servers. It is a bulletin board system, BBS, whereby people post (pin up) their thoughts, ideas, helpful suggestions, etc., and others can come along and look at what has been said and, if they wish, add their own comments.

Group naming conventions
The URLs of Usenet news are formatted similarly, but not identically, to other Web pages. For example, the URL `news:alt.tv.northern-exp` specifies the server protocol `news:` and the newsgroup `alt.tv.northern-exp`. Unlike other Internet connections, the URL does not need to specify a server name and pathname with preceding slashes. This is because the 'discussions' are held on separate news servers rather than at the sites of where people type in their discussion. We discuss this in more detail below.

Each newsgroup has a unique name, described with words separated by periods. Some words, *alt*, short for *alternative*, *comp*, for *computers, biz* for mainstream business topics and so on, specify a top-level category;

---

[2] Today, a number of search tools are using categories to make it easier for us to narrow our searches. See page 79 for details about Northern Light which specialises in this method of displaying matches to general keyword topics.

any following words specify a particular sub-group of that category.

How Usenet works

The process for retrieving information from news servers is significantly different to the process for retrieving information from World Wide Web servers. News messages[3] are collected and automatically distributed at periodic intervals, en masse, among news servers throughout the Usenet. When you supply a URL to request newsgroup messages, your request is routed to the news server, provided by your local service provider, which has accumulated messages throughout the Usenet system. In contrast, when you supply a URL to request a particular Web page, your request is routed to the single Web site whose server maintains and distributes that page.

A news message which you send goes to your local service provider's news server, whereupon the message is automatically distributed at periodic intervals to other participating Usenet news servers. Other Usenet readers can then access your news message but from their own local news server.

This batch processing of Usenet news permits an efficient distribution. For example, a popular Web site can get inundated with requests from all over the world for pages held at its site. In extreme cases, the server could even grind to a halt. However, a popular newsgroup is broadly distributed by the entire network of participating news servers. It is the local news server that handles requests but only from its own locality.

The diagram on page 54 shows a group of office computers connected to a switch box. This routes any request from a PC to the relevant server. If it is a newsgroup query, it goes to the local news server. This in

---

[3] Basically, these are similar to e-mail messages with no images or fancy text formatting.

turn is linked to other news servers world-wide, all of which are fed *news feeds* on a regular basis.

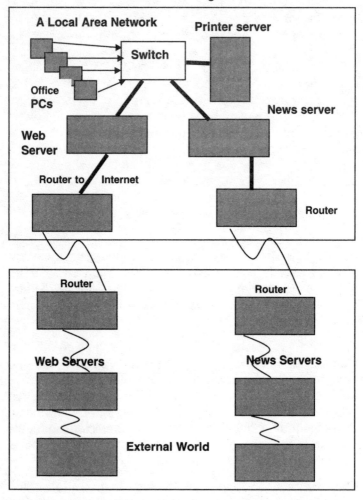

Figure 6.1: A LAN connected to the Internet via routers. Office PCs request services from the Switch server. These requests are forwarded to Printer, News or Web servers. Note that the Web and News servers are separate.

Chapter Summary:

We have looked at BBS and seen how to subscribe to them or at least read the discussions going on. These discussions can be simple fun, for example, during the 1998 World Cup, I followed a discussion about England's performance and what others thought of le Saux's tactics on the pitch. This could be golf, rugby, tennis, cricket, etc. I could have listened to the same sort of 'discussion' in my local pub, of course. But with Usenet, my 'local' became world-wide.

But there are also many discussions of a much more serious nature, perhaps some highly relevant to a given field of interest or research.

We also saw how a Usenet URL is different to a Web page URL because of the way news is gathered and circulated. News is fed to all *news servers* in Usenet at regular intervals. Each is maintained by a local service provider. But how many news groups that server can accommodate and for how long news messages are held depends on the service provider's resources. A Web site news specialist, such as Deja News, maintains many more newsgroups including some groups which local news servers have no access to.

Terms Used:

BBS	Bulletin Board System, same as Usenet
newsgroups	same as Usenet
protocol	an agreed common language used by servers with different operating systems so that each can understand the other. `news:` is the language or protocol agreed on by all news servers. `http` is the web server protocol

router	a device which routes data packets from one local area network (LAN) or wide area network (WAN) to another. Routers often serve as an Internet backbone, interconnecting all networks in the enterprise
subscribe	in the context of newsgroups, joining in a discussion group. There is no payment involved
thread	a topic or theme in a newsgroup discussion which generates on-going e-mail from interested parties
Usenet	Users Network - a discussion forum for people wishing to exchange ideas. Also called newsgroups

What is Next?

It looks as though we must have covered all the search tools available. But not so! There is one final and important set which we need to mention. Then, at last, we shall be in a position to use the WWW effectively for finding the information we want by knowing which is the right tool to use.

Some Things to Try

1. Visit Deja News and find out how to use it via the new users page - do note it is `shtml` !

```
http://www.dejanews.com/help/newusers.shtml
```

2. Try it out. See what people are saying about some topic of personal interest to you.

7:.. Recent & Helpful Specialist Tools

At last, we are on the final leg of our tour of searching tools. In this chapter, we shall look at some of the specialist ones available. These are tools which either specialise in searching for specific general topics, such as definitions of computer terms, train time tables, etc., or they are tools which specialise in the manner in which search queries can be entered or displayed.

What is presented below are a few of the specialist search tools which I have come across and which I hope may be of some interest and value to you. But there are many more which I have not yet come across or, if I have, have not had the time to explore. The main point is that *you* must be aware that such specialist tools exist, that *you* may need to actively search them out and once found, bookmark them in your browser for future use.

How do we come across them? Look in some of the daily newspapers which have Internet specials, such as the Times *Inter//face*, the Telegraph's *Connected,* the Guardian's *Online.* You may also come across them by reading books, magazines, and so on. Try asking colleagues which tools they use in the hope that they may refer to one that you have not used before but may find convenient.

AskJeeves™: This site allows you to enter questions in plain English, just as you would when asking a friend. It takes your query and lists a set of matching answers from its own database when possible. The user then selects the one closest to his/her needs. It will also search many other search tools and provide matches from their indexes. In other words, it behaves to some extent like an extended meta-search engine.

With other search engines it is up to you to browse through a list of matches or further refine your query to reduce the number of hits. This can be a long and frustrating exercise.

AskJeeves uses sophisticated natural language processing to understand and match users' queries. It has thousands of question templates and millions of researched answer-links to web sites and is increasing all the time. It also selects results from other search tools which closely match your query.

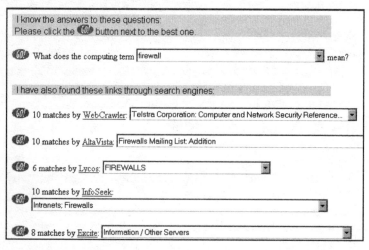

I wanted to know more about *firewalls*. After entering the query as: *"What is a firewall?"* the above was produced.

In this instance, it was able to produce an answer. My original question was reworded as:

What does the following computing term: firewall *mean?*

To the right is a down arrow (you can see some more in the illustration). Clicking on this will reveal a list of additional matches, as shown for the matches from AltaVista on page 59. Any one can be selected and then the *Go!* button to the left clicked to bring up that Web page.

Note that there are matches from other search engines: WebCrawler, AltaVista, Lycos, Infoseek and Excite.

Previously I had tried InfoSeek by simply entering the keyword 'firewall' in its main search facility. Infoseek gave 83,259 hits. Many of these were advertising their firewall programs. Not a nice task to have to sift through.

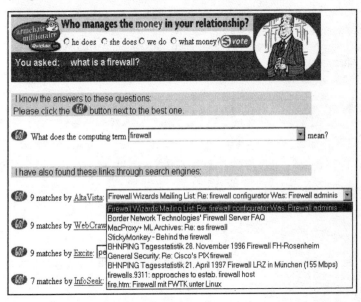

Fig: 7.1 Result of clicking on AltaVista's down arrow

AskJeeves gave me plenty of information and it was easy to select what was needed. This has now become one of my preferred ways of finding information. I know it is not perfect and there are certain subjects which I would prefer to search for using standard search engines, especially if I had to conduct research to any great depth. (To get a feel for how AskJeeves work, try typing in *world maps* as your query.)

Tech Web: Useful if you want to look up computing terms. At the time of writing it has some 11,000 computing terms and concept and is increasing all the time. If it cannot find a definition, it asks whether it should be added to its list. Try looking up the meaning of the terms *cookie* and *router*.

The ability to define terms is just a small part. It is a Web site which specialises in technology and provides the latest news about computing technology.

```
http://www.techweb.com:320/encyclopedia
```

New terms are listed. In the diagram below, it shows amongst others, 'nanny software' (in grey). Clicking on this, not only defined the term but also provided links to sites which offer programs to screen out Web pornography.

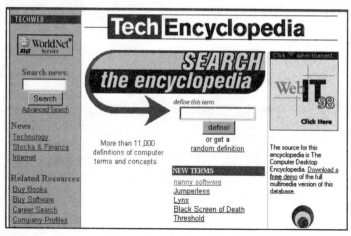

Copyright © 1998 CMP Media Inc.
Reproduced from *TechWeb* with permission.

Street maps: Another of my favourites is StreetMap. If you want a street map of your own locality in the UK, try this site:

```
http://www.streetmap.co.uk/
```

Maps may be customised and it is delightfully easy to use after a little experimentation. Streets, places of interest such as parks or buildings which appear on the map can be centred by clicking on a button. Once you have customised your map, it can be printed off.

World maps: Daily, more sites of interest are being offered. Do you want a map of the West Coast of Ireland? Then try this site:

```
http://mapweb.parc.xerox.com/
```

The list of sites providing maps of the world is too vast even to begin to summarise. (Try AskJeeves by entering *world maps* as your search query. When I did so, it returned a list of answers including reference maps, countries of the world, territorial maps, world cities, statistics for maps, map outlines, even European railroad maps. Under these were 8 matches from AltaVista, 10 from Yahoo!, 10 from WebCrawler, 3 from Excite and 3 from Lycos. Maps galore! It is quite breathtaking!)

People: WhoWhere? is an easy to use site for finding people's e-mail addresses. Simply type in a name. My own name appeared and that of a colleague. But other colleagues did not appear when I typed in their names. It would seem that one must have entered, at some time or other, one's e-mail address into the Web, perhaps, as in my case, because I have subscribed to various sites.

```
http://www.whowhere.com/
```

Businesses: Yell, one of the Internet Explorer's premier providers, also has a UK page which is an on-line version of Yellow Pages®. It is very simple to use. You can find out about plumbers or Italian restaurants in your own locality.

```
http://www.yell.co.uk/
```

NISS for library and educational matters: library OPACs in Higher Education; bookshops and publishers, other library resources, dictionaries, and other reference works, network directories, travel information, external data services, museums and galleries, ATHENS Subscription

Services, search engines. But I could not find a dictionary of quotations.

```
http://www.niss.ac.uk/reference/
```

Encyclopaedia Britannica: The Encyclopaedia Britannica is now on-line on the Web. If you are searching for certain topics, try it out. It has a free but limited search and encourages you and web authors to license it for your site.

'Subscribe' here *does* mean having to pay a subscription. I was given 38,781 matches for the question I entered in the search location box, *"What is the longest river in the world?"* Top of the list was the Yangtze river which is the third longest in the world but the longest in China and Asia. A fact which I had not asked for but nevertheless proved interesting. You can see that it was matching all of my keywords and also partial matches to my keywords.

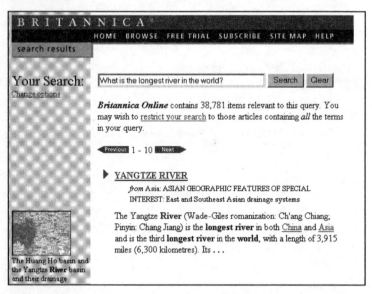

Underneath my question, is a paragraph inviting me to click on a phrase which will match all my keywords terms. I did so and Lo and behold! the first match in the list, now down to 157, gave me what I wanted. The longest river in the world being the Nile.

Of great interest too were the many other pages of relevant information. The fourth reference in this list was the Yangtze river which had originally come first. Another page referred to the five main drainage basins, and so on. Note too the map on the left.

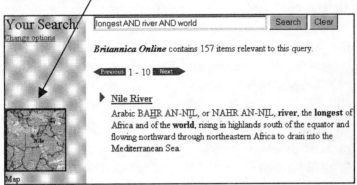

However, that is as far as I could get without having to subscribe to the Encyclopaedia at $85 per annum or $8.50 per month which I was asked for when I clicked on the map to get an enlarged version.

`http://www.eb.com/search/index.htcl` (Yes, that is HTCL).

World newspapers: From Netscape's News channel, you can select the world's newspapers or bookmark:

```
http://excite.netscape.com/directory/news/
world_newspapers
```

UK Weather from the Met office:
```
http://www.meto.govt.uk/sec3/sec3.html
```

Deja News for Usenet groups as discussed in detail on pages 50 - 51.

```
http://www.dejanews.com/
```

Train Times for Europe: Deutsche Bahn AG: An excellent place to check train times within the UK and Europe. Provides much more than times - connection stations, maps, on-line bookings, details of trains, for example, whether it has buffet facilities, sleepers, etc. It is worth trying.

```
http://bahn.hafas.de/english.html
```

Artists: For those who like paintings both new and old, try this site.

```
http://sunsite.doc.ic.ac.uk/wm/paint/auth/
```

It provides an extremely comprehensive list of well known painters. Thumbnail images are provided and enlarged versions obtained by clicking on the relevant thumbnail. For those in the UK, the Department of Computing at Imperial College, London, has a mirror Sunsite. The pictures are transferred at high speed since there is no need to contact the American Sunsite index.

Disqualified directors: From Companies House, this site provides information about disqualified directors, their addresses and reasons for disqualification.

```
http://www.companieshouse.gov.uk/
```

Alexa: Rely on Alexa's "Site Stats" information to help you make decisions about sites you visit while at work or at home. For example, you can learn which sites have been endorsed for electronic commerce before you hand out your credit card number. Or, find out how your company's Web site measures up to the competition in popularity. It speaks for itself!

It is not a search engine, but is worth trying out especially for businesses.

```
http://www.alexa.com/
```

Music: If you like music, try the following site. Northern Light has a special section for those interested in music. It has recently teamed up with Billboard Music Information

Search. It is simple to use. Just enter a name of an artist or composer, classical or pop. Sites with information about the person will be returned.

```
http://www.nlsearch.com/billboard/
```

Finally, try **Amnesi**: `http://www.amnesi.com/`
to find a URL for which you have forgotten the full address. Amnesi will find all matches to your partial entry. (Note it is AMNESI; another company has already taken AMNESIA!) The JavaScript is slow, but the results can be impressive. It also provides an information button to help you discover more about one of your selections.

Chapter Summary:
One is not restricted to using the standard search engines and directories offered by browsers and ISPs. There are many more search tools, some of which specialise in certain areas, time tables, street maps, encyclopaedia, general knowledge, etc. We have looked at a number of these specialised search tools. More are emerging all the time so keep yourself abreast of new developments.

Terms used:

JavaScript	a language, which has little to do with the Java programming language. It is embedded in Web pages to perform certain functions desired by Web authors
mirror site	another site holding identical data to a base site, usually in another country to allow faster access to the data from that country

What is Next?
In the next chapter, we shall examine the subject of advanced searching techniques. These are techniques used by the canny searcher when he/she wishes to reduce a huge list of results to a manageable and more relevant number. It is easy to learn and after some practice, easy to use. We shall also look at the use of advanced forms

which allow users to perform advanced searches without the need for knowing these techniques.

Some Things to Try

Select one or more of the search tools mentioned and try them out. Some contain many more features than I have covered in the brief descriptions. If you like music, try:

```
http://www.nlsearch.com/billboard
```

8: Advanced Searching

How to enter search keywords

One final matter. To become an experienced web searcher one must learn the techniques of advanced searching. The objective of this section is to show how we can reduce a large number of hits to a manageable number by using advanced searching features. For example, using one search engine to find *"consultancy jobs in Civil Engineering"* produced 1,815,771 hits. Monstrous! However, by using advanced features and restricting my search to *Northern California*, it came down to a mere 44. Very few extra keystrokes were involved.

jobs consulting engineer civil: 1,815,771 hits

**+jobs +consulting +engineer +civil +"Northern California":
44 hits**

Note the inclusion of plus signs (+) and double quotes ("). That was all that was required to reduce it to a manageable size of hits. Some old hands[1] frequently type in their keywords without any advanced features simply to get some idea of what they are up against. Then, they begin to refine and narrow their search to a manageable size.

It takes a little practice but is a must for serious Web searchers. In my early days, I once tried *bridge*, meaning the card game bridge. It came at the bottom of a list of over 20,000. All the others were to do with all the bridges in the world. If I had known then about advanced features, I would have been able to reduced this number significantly.

Introduction to Advanced Searching Techniques

Search providers frequently bemoan "the lazy and sloppy attitudes" of their users when entering keywords and the

---

[1]   An 'old hand' would not be more than four years old! There are very few people around with even four years experience of professional searching on the Web.

fact that few use advanced features. A little investment of your time and a bit of practice will pay dividends by reducing the hours spent and the resulting frustration of searching through a quagmire of hits.

Each search tool has its own set of rules for using advanced features and, therefore, you should become familiar with your own favourite tool. Most search tools have a *help* or *tips* page on how to enter advanced features for their particular engine. It is worth printing these off and studying them.

Techniques for Entering Keyword Terms

Simple searches

Most search tools allow users to enter words or phrases as *keywords* or as *natural language*.

Example of *keywords*: Alzheimer's, inheritance

Example of *natural language*: Inheritance of Alzheimer's

Usually, commas are ignored by search tools, but they can be added for clarity when typing. Common words such as "*the, web, cgi[2], text, of, HTML*" and special characters *(& , - : /)*, with the exception of the period, are usually ignored by most search tools. Entering these so-called *stop-words* will return no matches for them.

The reason why *jobs consulting engineer civil:* gives 1,815,771 hits is because it finds all documents in its index where all or some or even just one of the words appear. This is why the number of hits keeps increasing as each new word is added.

jobs: - 589,971
jobs consulting: - 1,045,183
jobs consulting engineer: 1,327,398
jobs consulting engineer civil: 1,815,771

---

[2] Common Gateway Interface: the protocol used by programs which process data entered into Web forms.

Of course, most search tools should list those hits with all four words at the top unless concept matching is also involved.

Simple keyword searches can be converted into advanced searches by merely adding symbols (+, - ") or by using the following words: AND, OR, NOT.

Advanced features
All search tools have advanced features, although many vary in exactly how they should be used. It is important to become accustomed to how your own favourite tool expects advanced features to be used. All search tools have a *Tips* or *How to Enter Advanced Features* page. Take time to read this page. It will pay handsome dividends. Most, if not all, have the following features in common but there will be subtle differences. So this is a general guide.

Plus Sign (+): This means that the word the plus sign is attached to *must* appear in the document. It is placed in front of the word *with no space between the sign and the word*.

> *Example: Pets +cats +dogs* would pick up any document with *pets* as optional and *cats* and *dogs* as mandatory.

Minus sign (-): This sign means do not find documents with this word in. Like the plus sign it must go in front of the word with no space.

> *Example: +billiards -supplies -equipment* would pick up documents with billiards in but you would be spared those which relate to supplies and equipment, unless a supplier pays to have an advert with the search provider.

Quotes (Phrase): "Northern California" If you wish to search for a phrase, then most search tools recognise the double quotes. It means: "find documents which contain the phrase in quotes in the exact order given". Without the quotes, the search tool would find all documents with either or both words *Northern* and *California*.

> *Example:* "Rock Hudson" would find documents in which Rock Hudson the film star appears. Without quotes, I would get any document which has the word *rock* or *Hudson* in it or both.

Double quotes are useful when searching for proper names, company names, titles, regional names, etc.

Using AND, OR and AND NOT
These are the three so-called Boolean operators. They must be written with *a space on either side*.

AND: Documents found must contain all words joined by the word AND. Similar to the plus sign.

> *Example:* "Wizard AND Oz AND movie" would find documents in which the three words appear.

OR: Documents found must contain at least one of the words joined by OR.

> *Example:* "cat OR kitten" would find documents with either (or both) words *cat* or *kitten*. But do not be surprised if Mistress Kitten's adult page is amongst them!

AND NOT: Documents to be found must not contain the words. Similar to the minus sign. Frequently, it is written simply as NOT.

> *Example*: "pets AND NOT snakes".

Some search tools, for example, Excite, require the Boolean operators to be typed in uppercase. It is always safe to use uppercase. Northern Light limits the number of Boolean operators to one. Some search tools do not recognise them, for example, Yahoo! and InfoSeek. Whereas all the major search tools allow the use of the plus and minus signs. You can now see why you need to read the searching tips for your preferred search tool.

Advanced Searching Made Easier Using Forms
Today, many search tools provide an advanced entry form which can be filled in rather than using the above symbols. Each differs slightly, especially in the words used. But it is simple to work out. The keywords are typed into the boxes and the down arrows used to select the various options.

Here is a typical example, it comes from Excite:

Each search engine has slightly different options. The InfoSeek advanced form has some choices not given by Excite. For example, a search, and this could be useful for researchers, can be limited to one of the main domains: *com* (commercial/profit making), *gov* (government), *edu* (educational), etc. Summaries may be shown or hidden and the number of results limited to 10, 20, 25 or 50.

In the InfoSeek form there is also a *Search by collection* box which refers to the entire Web or one of the Web guides such as sports, entertainment, automotives, etc. The *Search by location* box limits the search to a particular

71

country or the entire World Wide Web (*Earth* in InfoSeek-speech).

You need to become accustomed to how each tool provides its own advanced searching. AltaVista has a *refine* box. Asking for musical instruments gave me a list of over 3 million. By clicking on the *refine* box, these were categorised, some of which are shown in the following.

Refine your search by requiring a few relevant topics, excluding irrelevant ones, and ignoring the others.
GRAPH ▶

Search   Refine Again

73% **Musical**, instruments, music, instrument, musicians, composers, composer

26% **Piano**, pianos, pianist

26% **Percussion**, drums, ensemble, drum, ensembles, keyboards, snare, cymbal

26% **Guitar**, guitars, bass, acoustic

23% **Sound**, midi, sounds, synthesizer, synthesizers, sequencer, reverb, playback, sequencers

22% **Orchestra**, orchestral, Symphony, orchestras, Concerto, Sonata, conductor, Concertos, Sonatas

22% **Band**, bands, marching

Rather than using advanced forms, experienced searchers would find it faster and easier to use symbols and Boolean operators, so it is worth getting used to them.

A HotBot Special

The person: Selecting this and typing *Zeppo Marx* would return any of the following:

Zeppo Marx   Mr. Zeppo Marx   Marx Zeppo.

In other search tools, use the quotes method.

Summary of Advanced Searching
Let us try to summarise the above and make it more simple. The first thing to do once you have chosen a search engine or directory that suits your style and demands, is to learn more about how that search tool works. Use any button that appears to provide users with more help. A *Tips* or *Help* link is typical. An *Advanced*

search link will, in some cases, take you directly to an advanced form rather than a help page. You will need to experiment with each tool. Most search engines will accept the following:

Symbol	Meaning
" quotes" e.g.: "X Y Z"	a phrase that must be found and in the order given
+ in front of a word with no space between the + and the word.	this word MUST be included Equivalent to AND
- in front of a word with no space between the - and the word.	This word must not be included. Equivalent to NOT (or AND NOT)
spaces between words	One or more of the words must be found. Equivalent to OR
* any characters after the letters. e.g. nurs*	would include nurse, nurses, nursing. Not common!
Case sensitive	some search tools are case sensitive. Always use lowercase except for proper names

Additional Features offered by some Search Tools

Case Sensitivity: Some search tools, for example AltaVista, are case sensitive which means that some will produce different results for the word *entertainment* and *Entertainment*. Some people spend a great deal of wasted effort worrying about this and begin to put in all possible variations, for example:

entertainment, Entertainment, ENTERTAINMENT, enTERtainment

It gets worse for phrases like *golf courses, GOLF courses, golf COURSES, Golf Courses,* etc., etc. And then what about singular and plural forms?

So what can we do? The simple answer is to relax and always enter words in lowercase. Most search tools will match lowercase entries with any uppercase variation.

There is one situation where lowercase may not be appropriate with some search tools and that is where you have used quotes. For example, "world health organisation" may match only lowercase.

Variations on Words
Using the truncation symbol asterisk (*) can match a variety of words. For example, *nurs** should match: *nurse*, *nurses*, *nursing*, etc. But only a few search tools accept the asterisk, e.g., Yahoo! and AltaVista.

Field searching
Many search tools allow you to search for your keywords which appear **only** in the *titles* of Web documents or in the *body* of a document. Northern Light, AltaVista, HotBot and InfoSeek are examples. The idea here is that if your keywords have been entered in a title, then it must be highly relevant. Other fields are "text" and "url".

Simply add `text:` or `title:` followed by your keywords. `'title:your keywords'` will find pages with those keywords in titles or `'text:your keywords'` - to find your keywords only in the main body of pages.

Serious researchers may wish to limit their searches to those web pages emanating from certain organisations. This they can do using a field search on a URL.

`url:searchenginewatch.com`

`url:nasa.gov title:pathfinder` would find all pages on NASA servers with *Pathfinder* in the page title.

Some Examples
The more terms used the narrower the search should be provided that the plus sign (or Boolean AND) is used. Words by themselves will merely increase the number of hits, as shown earlier.

Search Query	No. of Hits
Auto parts BMW	1,562,106
"auto parts" +BMW	511,410

Search Query	No. of Hits
bridge AND games	1,400,000+
game +bridge	336510
"bridge game"	770

Comparing search engines using the same queries

Excite: search query	No. of Hits
world health organisation	1,921,789
"world health organisation"	3803
+world +health +organisation	3340 (but not quite the same set as phrase search results above. The first one had nothing to do with WHO)
AND world AND health AND organisation	none

AltaVista	
world health organisation	4,444,770
"world health organisation"	10,463
+world +health +organisation	71,146 relevant to WHO
AND world AND health AND organisation	none, required use of advanced search link

InfoSeek	
world health organisation	14,613,455
"world health organisation"	18,787 highly relevant but did include "Global Health"

Chapter Summary:

We have seen that simple searches can result in a large numbers of hits but by the use of advanced searching techniques, these can be cut down to a more manageable size.

We have looked at many of the advanced features, such as special symbols and Boolean operators as well as advanced searching via forms. Which is better? An experienced searcher would find it faster to enter the special symbols and Boolean operators rather than filling out a form. But, in the end, it is your choice.

Terms used:

advanced searching	techniques using symbols and Boolean operators to narrow the search range
Boolean operators	AND, OR & NOT AND - these limit query strings so that a search can be narrowed
stop words	words ignored in search query strings, such as *the*, *HTML*, *web*
truncation symbol	usually, the asterisk. It is used as a wildcard character to match variation. For example, *nurs** would match with *nurse*, *nursing* and *nurses*. Used only with some search tools

What is next?

In the next chapter, we shall summarise what we have learnt in all the preceding chapters. Through some examples we shall see which of the tools may be the most suitable ones to use.

Some Things to Try

1. Conduct a survey of your own by comparing the number of hits from various search tools when the same search query is entered. Experiment with some of the advanced features too. For example, try: `+billiards +rules` for the rules of the game. This may help you to find your favourite.

2. Now that we have covered all the main topics, those who would like to find more detailed information should try the following sites. This is for the really serious:

`http://searchenginewatch.com/webmasters/features.html`

`http://www.windweaver.com/searchguide.htm` (**not** html)

Browsing through these pages will lead you to many more pages on related topics.

9: Which Tool to Choose?

We have finally completed our tour of the various search tools available to us and seen that there are many to choose from, but which one? That really depends on what you are searching for. We shall summarise the types of various tools available and then look at some examples by which we can contrast various approaches.

Summary of searching Tools

Meta-search engines: If you are a beginner, this is a good place to start. Various search engines and directories are enlisted automatically by a meta-search engine. See page 24 for more details. Experienced searchers use these tools when they are not sure where to begin or when they want a general feel for what is out on the Web.

Search engines and/or Directories: Once you have come across your favourite search tool, bookmark it so that you have a quick and easy method of accessing it. Northern Light is my current favourite, because of its categorisation methodology. AltaVista, HotBot, Excite are highly popular search engines, each with its own unique flavour. Yahoo!, LookSmart and Snap! are all highly recommended directories, the latter becoming a must for the teenager community. Remember that one tool may well be partnered with or have affiliations with other tools. So you may well be using more than one search tool. See page 23 for details of these partnerships so that you do not duplicate your time and effort. Remember too that should your favourite not present what you want, try one of the others.

Web channels should be used for certain topics which come under more general headings such as news, jobs, travel, entertainment, health, stock and shares, weather. Such information can be found very quickly.

Newsgroups may also be rewarding if you want to see what others think and say about things. Using Deja News during the World Cup of 1998, and typing in "*World Cup, le Saux*" I was taken into a series of 'discussions' about what people thought about his performance. It is all highly personal and more like the 'discussions' heard in pubs. However, it can prove entertaining and you can always add your two-penn'orth. For more serious matters a real debate might be taking place with up-to-date findings of what is happening world wide.

Specialist search tools such as AskJeeves, TechWeb, Deutsche Bahn AG, etc., see Chapter 7, are highly relevant tools and may well provide your answers more quickly than by using the standard search engines and directories. I frequently make use of AskJeeves when I am not sure of which search tool to use or when I want some information quickly. It is also an extremely good place for beginners.

It is up to you to decide which search tool is more relevant at any given time. And you can make that decision only after you have gained experience in their use.

An Example:
Let us take the following as an example.

I wanted information about *blood pressure*. I typed in the keywords using Excite and got 939,629 hits. Far too many, so I then added the words *heart* and *disease* using advanced features and the list dropped to 1880.

```
+blood +pressure +heart +disease
```

With Yahoo! I got 34 with the words *blood pressure* ; adding *heart disease* got this down to 11. Not bad.

Bear in mind that Excite gives its top ten first, that is, those which most closely match your keywords based on their internal ranking algorithm. These might well be highly relevant.

In the case of Yahoo!, because their listings are created by humans, the fact that only 11 were given may not matter. It meant they were all highly relevant to my requirements.

I then tried Northern Light. The advantage of Northern Light is that it works out a data structure and presents the user with an organised list of hits and not just from pages on the Web but from other sources too, called their *Special Collection*.

At least that is what the blurb said, so I just had to try it out. I entered 'blood pressure' and got some 199,066 hits. Alongside each listing was an additional flag saying whether it belongs to the WWW or to the Special Collection. Still very large, but on the left side of the screen a list of categories appeared. The first column in the table below is the folder categories listed when *blood pressure* was typed in.

Blood Pressure	Heart Disease
Special Collection documents	Special Collection documents
Hypertension	Angina
Commercial sites	Commercial sites
Heart (Physiology)	MDX Health Digest (article summaries)
Cardiovascular system	British Medical Journal
Heart disease	Government sites
MDX Health Digest (article summaries)	mediconsult.com
Personal pages	Non-profit sites
Government sites	www.healthtouch.com
Vitamins	Lancet (magazine)
Weightlifting	www.bmj.com
Cardiology	www.aomega.com
all others...	all others...

Highly impressed, I selected the *Heart disease* category. A new set of folders appeared, those shown in column 2, some containing categories from the previous list. There were 1673 hits. I also tried the *Special Collection*. That contained 431 hits from a wide variety of sources. I chose one and got a summary and a well documented account of the source. This was free. If I were interested, a charge was also listed ($1 for the two-page article) for the full document. If I paid a monthly fee of $4.95, I would be entitled to 50 free documents each month.

For the serious researcher especially in business and medicine, this will be a small price to pay for information.

Below is the result of entering 'aphids'. Note the list of categories to the left. All the documents shown are from the WWW. Those from the *Special Collection* would be flagged as such.

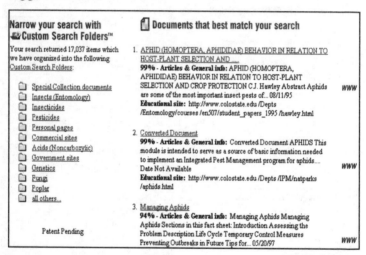

Until we explore all the various search tools we cannot make an informed decision as to which one suits us best. One experienced association recommends all search tools but has a favourite list for general Web searching comprising: AltaVista Advanced Search[1], InfoSeek and Northern Light.

---

[1] Advanced searching is described in Chapter 8.

Finally, I chose AskJeeves. The following was in response to *blood pressure.*

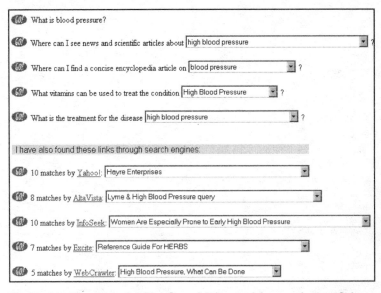

Plenty to get started with. So which would you choose? It depends on how deeply you wish to research some topic. AskJeeves is a good starting place. Northern Light is an excellent site if you need to home into a particular aspect of some topic.

Northern Light was launched in August, 1997. It claimed to be different to other Search Engines because it categorises its lists. It provides a free Web search as well as a Special Collection comprising material from books, magazines, databases and news articles and journals. You have to pay for the Special Collection averaging at about $1. They have a money back guarantee if not 100% satisfied with your findings and no hassle! This unique collection has over 5000 sources and rising with each month. Its main target is the business market both small and home businesses as well as a general search tool for everyday web users.

10: Useful URLs

Here are some useful Web site addresses, many of which have been discussed in the text.

Note: add `http://` to all URLs and note that not all of them begin with www

Site	URL
Alexa: provides useful information about the sites you are viewing	`widener.alexa.com/`
AltaVista	`www.altavista.digital.com/`
Amnesi	`www.amnesi.com/`
anti-porn sites for parents	`www.netparents.org/start/`
AskJeeves	`www.askjeeves.com/`
AskJeeves for Kids	`www.ajkids.com/`
Berkeley University: Very useful site for information about search tools for the beginner and for Web authors	`library.berkeley.edu/TeachingLib/Guides/Internet/` & `www.lib.berkeley.edu/TeachingLib/Guides/Internet/ToolsTables.html`
Businesses, UK:	`www.yell.co.uk/`
Cyber Patrol	`www.cyberpatrol.com/`
CyberSitter	`www.solidoak.com/index.html`
Deja News	`www.dejanews.com/`
Disney Internet Guide	`www.disney.com/`
disqualified directors	`www.companieshouse.gov.uk/`
DogPile	`www.dogpile.com/`
Encyclopedia Britannica	`www.eb.com/search/index.htcl` (Yes! that is `'htcl'`)
European train times	`bahn.hafas.de/english.html`
Excite	`www.excite.com/`
FBI: safety tips for children	`www.fbi.gov/kids/internet/internet.htm` (not html)
GoTo.com	`www.goto.com/`
Inference Find	`www.inference.com/infind/`
InfoSeek	`www.infoseek.com/`
Internet World	`www.iw.com/`
LookSmart	`www.looksmart.com/`

Site	URL
Lycos	www.lycos.com/
Lycos SafetyNet	personal.lycos.com/safetynet/ safety.asp
MetaCrawler	www.metacrawler.com/
Metafind	www.metafind.com/
music - Northern Light has a special section for those interested in music. NL has recently teamed up with Billboard Music Information Search	www.nlsearch.com/billboard/
NISS for education	www.niss.ac.uk/reference/
Northern Light	www.northernlight.com/
painters	sunsite.doc.ic.ac.uk/wm/paint /auth/
Search Engine Watch	www.searchenginewatch.com/ & www.searchenginewatch.com/ whatsnew.html
Snap!	www.snap.com/
street maps: UK	www.streetmap.co.uk/
SurfWatch	www.surfwatch.com/
TechWeb	www.techweb.com:320/encyclopedi a
weather: UK	www.meto.govt.uk/sec3/sec3.html
WhoWhere?	www.whowhere.com/
Windweaver: tips for Web authors	www.windweaver.com/ searchguide.htm (not HTML)
world maps	mapweb.parc.xerox.com/
world newspapers	excite.netscape.com/directory/ news/world_newspapers/
Yahoo!	www.yahoo.com/
Yahooligans!	www.yahooligans.com/

11: Notes for Web Authors & Web Masters

The following are some notes and useful tips for those who are serious Web authors and Web masters.

Web Authors & Web Masters

By default, the first 200 characters of a web page are used as a summary by many search engines in their returned matches. Therefore, important keywords should appear within the first 200 characters forming part of the main heading and first paragraph. If keywords are not in this summary, then a user may not bother to click on your page. Many of the 'best pages' do not get into the top 10 because authors do not enter important keywords in their first 200 characters.

Authors need to be aware that the use of tables and JavaScript may result in their first paragraph being pushed down the page and, therefore not appear in the summary.

Tables are how a browser will display a page on the screen, but the search engine will not see it like that. For example, a two column table with a contents list in column one and the descriptive paragraphs in column two will be 'seen' by search engines as two single columns. Column 1 being followed by column 2. Your wonderful 'opening' paragraph will no longer appear in the first 200 characters.

Contents	
Pet care	**Taking care of your pet** A dog is not just for Christmas Day but for all 365 days of the year.
Wildlife creatures	If you find an injured creature, approach it with care. Remember that it will be in pain and frightened by your approach.
etc.....	etc..

What a browser will display.

Contents
Pet care
Wildlife creatures
etc......
Taking care of your pet
A dog is not just for Christmas Day but for all 365 days of the year.
If you find an injured creature, approach it with care. Remember that it will be in pain and frightened by your approach.
etc..

A search engine will see the page as a series of columns in consecutive order.

Likewise, adding JavaScript before an opening paragraph will 'push' the paragraph down the page.

You can specify a different description by including it within meta tags. InfoSeek, AltaVista, HotBot and WebCrawler are meta tag enabled search engines. Add a description tag, up to 200 characters in length, and a keyword tag, up to a 1000 characters.

```
<meta name="description" content="enter your
200 character description here">
```

Specify keywords as follows:

```
<meta name="keywords" content="enter your
1000 character keywords here">
```

It is worth putting in sensible keywords in your <TITLE> tags and <META> tags. Many search engines will crawl pages and add words found there to their index. They may also increase the ranking of such pages so that there is a greater chance such pages appearing near the top of a list.

Words used in the descriptive meta, title tags and the first 200 words of your web pages are important because they are returned as the summary information of search tools' results. A good opening paragraph and concise meta tags are keys to creating good summaries. But not all search engines look at meta tags! So, you will still need to have a good opening paragraph.

If you had a page about stamp collecting, 'stamps' alone would not be a good keyword. Add: *stamp collecting, stamp collectors, stamps as a hobby, old stamps, current stamps,* etc., and even *philately* to your meta and title tags as well as the opening paragraph.

for more information try:

```
http://northernwebs.com/set/set06.html
```

Beware of putting keywords in as graphics. They may look pretty but search engines cannot 'read them'.

Avoid 'spamming', otherwise your pages may become penalised. Search engines are beginning to wise up to the tricky methods employed by spammers. For example, by entering same keywords as lines of text where the text is either in the same colour as the background or in a tiny font.

If your page has changed and you think a new abstract is in order, fill out the *'add URL form'* telling the search engine to re-visit your site. This is particularly necessary for Lycos.

Make sure that your home page contains links to other important pages. Remember, too, that links in *frames* and *image maps* may not be searched by some search engines. Many search engines will not follow links in *frame* and *frameset* tags, and may be ignored altogether. If you are using frames, start using the *noframes* tag to provide an alternative for these engines.

Remember, too, that a site with good content is more likely to be reviewed and re-visited by directory editors.

Web masters
URLs may be quite intimidating to a novice, difficult to type or even to read. With a little thought, web masters can

create less intimidating URLs as well as ones which are easier to type and read.

Magazine publishers have found that some characters used in URLs are also used in typesetting and have particular meanings. The tilde (~) is one example of character which has to be specially marked in order to be included in the printed form. Forgetting to do so results in it disappearing from the printed text. Backquotes (') and the percentage symbol (%) are two more.

Certain other characters can be notoriously difficult to typeset in certain fonts. The tilde can be mistaken for a quotation mark. Other characters can be misleading, example:

digit zero "0" and uppercase *Oh* "O";
digit one (1) and the letter *el* (l).

What is the following character? (I). It is actually, uppercase "i". See RFC 1738 for the syntax for URLs[1]. The underscore character is one of my pet hates, especially when it is underlined as hypertext!

Who has not cursed at the length of some URLs?

A URL should try to reflect the actual name of an organisation for those who have forgotten the URL and are making a stab at it. (See page 90.)

Consistency in folder names should also be considered. Course notes from the 'Maths' department under a folder *Maths* should be consistent with course notes from the 'Physics' department under a folder *Physics* rather than some other named folder called *PH*.

For more information try the following by Paul E. Hoffman.

```
http://info.isoc.org/HMP/PAPER/016/html/
paper.html
```

---

[1] Syntax for URLs. Berners-Lee, et al. "Uniform Resource Locators (URL) RFC 1738. ftp://ds.internic.net/rfc/rfc1738.txt

A really Big Tip

Search Engine Watch, is a site maintained by Danny Sullivan, for the Mecklermedia Corporation. He is an Internet consultant, writer, and recognised search engine expert. It was created for the benefit of both search engine users and web developers. See the home page for full details:

http://searchenginewatch.com/

A monthly e-mail companion, free of charge, called *Search Engine Report* provides a wealth of informed information. Changes to search engines, new search tools, statistics, and hot 'gossip' - which search engine has fallen out with whom and which is getting into bed with another.

Anyone interested in what is going on, what lies ahead, unbiased reports on the value of the latest changes to existing search tools, evaluation of new ones, etc., should not waste a moment in joining this site and getting the monthly e-mail. It should be required reading for web authors and web masters.

It was in the July edition, number 20, that I came across a feature on how teachers and parents can prevent their children from being exposed to porn. In the same edition, two new services which had just come out in the previous month were also reviewed.

Web masters may also be interested in:

http://searchenginewatch.com/webmasters/
features.html

Another site of interest to web authors and masters is the Internet World at: http://www.iw.com/

Here you can keep up to date with Internet and Web development in general.

Also try the Windweaver site at:

```
http://www.windweaver.com/searchguide.htm
```

that is `htm` - not `html`, but note the confusion this can cause!

Have you ever wondered why the URL for AltaVista is **not** `www.altavista.com` **but** `www. altavista.digital.com` ?

When AltaVista made its debut in 1995, no one checked whether the *altavista.com* domain name was in use. It was! by AltaVista Technologies, Inc.®. According to Search Engine Report, No: 21, this oversight may cost Compaq which recently purchased Digital, the parent company of AltaVista, $3 million to rectify. Digital had a sub-domain name: *altavista.digital.com* where AltaVista was originally placed.

For years, AltaVista Technologies, Inc has been getting visits and, consequently, publicity from people typing in the wrong URL, as I did recently.

Note that I came across this little snippet by reading the *Search Engine Report*. I would recommend every web author and web master to subscribe to this highly informative publication. After all, it is free!

12: For Parents & Teachers
The Porn Problem

We do not have to dwell on the problems facing parents and teachers on how to prevent their children being faced with pornography over the Web.

Searching on the keyword 'porn' will bring a multitude of web pages from many web sites. Worse, one can be searching for some innocent topic only to find porn pages being included in the returned matches.

Clicking on any *Adult* button, even from the main browser companies, will provide pictures of material which magazines would not be allowed to publish.

One teacher was dismayed to find porn material at the top of a list whilst searching for material in front of her class pupils. One of many similar stories! So what can be done?

The bad news is that nothing will be 100% safe. The good news is that much can be done to lessen the problem. There are two basic approaches to the solution. One is to restrict children to those services which allow access only to web pages which have been carefully reviewed by search providers' editors. Reviewing sites is time consuming, of course, and, consequently, the knowledge base is limited. Worse, it cannot prevent children using some other 'adult' service.

The second approach is to employ programs, such as SurfWatch. These block access to over 100,000 sites which specialise in explicit sex, violence, hate speech, gambling, drugs and alcohol.

Children's Sites
Of late, many search providers offer 'kid-friendly' search services. These work in the different ways mentioned above. Some provide a filtering technology, such as Lycos's SafteyNet. This filters objectionable material from

the top search results and prevents adult-orientated adverts from being loaded. It looks for words which are common to adult material and pushes these pages to the end of the search results, where they are less likely to be found. But it is not perfect.

In contrast to SafetyNet, other services, especially directory services such as Yahoo!'s *Yahooligans!* and *Disney Internet Guide* (DIG for short), hand pick sites for inclusion in their service. Since these are filtered by humans, they are less likely to allow objectionable material to be included in their results.

AskJeeves for Kids is another site orientated towards children. It employs both approaches. There is the *Ask Jeeves for Kids* knowledge base containing carefully reviewed web pages. Secondly, it has the AskJeeves for Kids Metasearch service which retrieves matches from the major search tools but employs *SurfWatch* to filter the results.

Where to Find More Information
Any of these could become your home page, see details in Appendix A, page 100, or look for the *Make it your home page* link in the relevant web page.

AskJeeves for Kids
http://www.ajkids.com/

Yahooligans!
http://www.yahooligans.com/

Disney Internet Guide
http://www.disney.com/

Lycos SafetyNet - details at:
http://personal.lycos.com/safetynet/safetynet.asp

For many more sites
http://www.netparents.org/start/

Lists many other sites which provide services for children.

A parents organisation - USA based
http://www.netparents.org/
or Email: webmaster@netparents.org /

Safety Tips from the FBI
http://www.fbi.gov/kids/internet/internet.htm

Filtering Programs
SurfWatch
http://www.surfwatch.com/

CyberSitter
http://www.solidoak.com/index.html

Cyber Patrol
http://www.cyberpatrol.com/

Out of interest here is what TechWeb[1] supplied in its definition of *nanny software*.

"Parental Control Software
A program designed to screen out Web sites that feature pornography and other material not suited for young children and teenagers. The techniques vary, but most such programs use keyword lists and a continuously-updated database of Web sites that have been reviewed by the developer. Leading programs include Cyber Patrol, CyberSitter, Net Nanny, Net Shepherd, and SurfWatch.

One of the best sources of information on these and other programs is the Netparents Web site at www.netparents.org."

This shows how contacting one site can lead to reference sources elsewhere.

---

[1] From the TechWeb site. Source is acknowledged.

Personalisation Pages

To keep you locked on to their site, many search providers offer a personalised (personalized) search page. After entering registration details, etc., this page can contain some matters of personal interest. For example, Excite offers a choice of daily cartoons, a horoscope, local weather, access to chat groups, top news stories, crosswords and other word puzzles, and so on. This may prove useful for some.

You make your own choice of cartoons, news topics and so on.

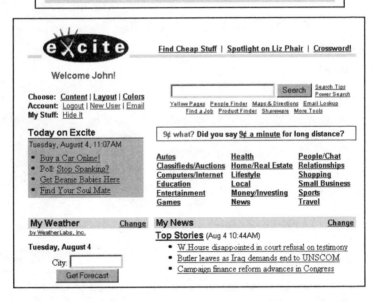

The above shows my own personalised page from Excite. It contains more than just my name. It has my regional weather forecast, a selection of cartoons - my choice of them, my horoscope, etc., most of which lie below the screen shot shown.

Appendix A
How to Use your Browser

We look at a typical browser, Netscape, and discuss some of the features of general interest. Most of the features are found in all versions of Netscape and Internet Explorer.

The Title Bar
This provides the name of the browser as well as the title of the Web page being displayed. This title, if it exists, is picked up from <TITLE> tag supplied by the author of the Web page; otherwise, some browsers will display the location of the page.

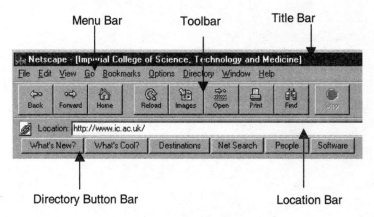

Menu Bar   Toolbar   Title Bar

Directory Button Bar   Location Bar

The Menu Bar
Allows access to all the menu commands. Here are some of the more frequently used commands.

File
Open File: opens a web page stored on your own hard disc as opposed to a site server. Used when creating one's own web page.

Page Setup: what you want to see when printing web pages; for example:

Print: selects printer and sends page off for printing. If frames are being used in the web page, this changes to

Print Frame: but make sure that you have clicked in the frame you want to print.

Save As: saves a copy of the web page on your hard disc. Not very useful since images may not be saved. Better to use *Bookmark* (see below).

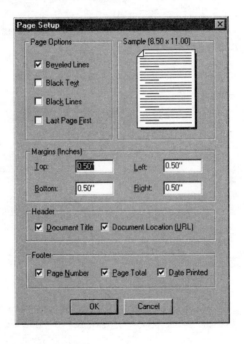

Edit

Select All (Ctrl+A): useful, especially in *Document Source* (*View* menu) to select the entire source code of the web page.

Find: finds words in the web page. Useful if you wish to locate a word or phrase in a large web page, saves having to scroll.

The *Edit* menu also has the *copy, cut & paste* features. However, if you are trying to copy source code (see below) so that you can paste it into a Word document, you are advised to use the Ctrl+C (copy) method. That is what Netscape advises! Then use Ctrl+V to paste. Do not forget that Ctrl+A will select all the text and then apply the Ctrl+C to copy it to the clipboard.

View
The first two are useful ones for HTML authors.

Document Source which will open a new window and reveal the web source code.

Document Information provides details about the URLs, images, etc.

Go: allows menu access to go back or forwards to other web pages you have visited. Seldom used because these actions are buttons on the Toolbar.

Refresh (Not on Macintosh): brings a fresh copy of the current Netscape page from local memory to replace the one originally loaded. The refreshed page does not display changes made to the source page from the time of the original loading.

Reload: brings a fresh copy of the current Netscape page to replace the one originally loaded. Netscape checks the network server to see if any change to the page has occurred. If there is no change, the fresh copy is retrieved from the cache. (See page 103 for details about how the cache works.) If there is a change, the fresh copy is transmitted from the network server and the reloaded page displays the updated page contents.

If you press the *Reload* button while holding down the Shift key (*Option* key on Macintosh), Netscape retrieves a fresh version from the network server regardless of whether the page has been updated. The cache is not used.

Bookmarks

The *Add Bookmark* will add the current web page to a list of bookmarks. This is a quick way of re-visiting a site's web page without having to type in the URL in the Location box. Simply click the required bookmark from the list.

The *Go to Bookmarks* displays a dialogue box listing all the bookmarks. When the list of bookmarks in the *Bookmark* menu exceeds 23, use this option. It is also used when you want to delete bookmarks. Highlight the bookmark(s) to delete and simply press the *Delete* key on your keyboard.

Options

This allows you to control what toolbars to show, colours for links and text, starting page, etc. It is worth exploring these and to use the help button for more information about each of the options.

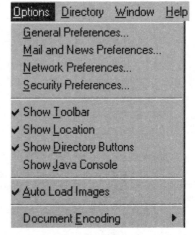

General Preferences: produce the various options shown in Figure A.1. It is worth exploring them.

The *Show* section turns on or off the various bars.

Auto Load Images: will load and display images if it has a tick mark. If there is no tick, images are not loaded and this will speed up the overall display of the page.

You can later click on the *Images* button on the Toolbar if you want to see the images.

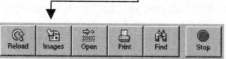

In the following dialogue box which appears when the *General Preferences* option is chosen, there are tabs for each set of options. *Appearance* and *Colors* are two we shall look at. The *Colors* tab is shown below. You can choose colours for the text, background and links.

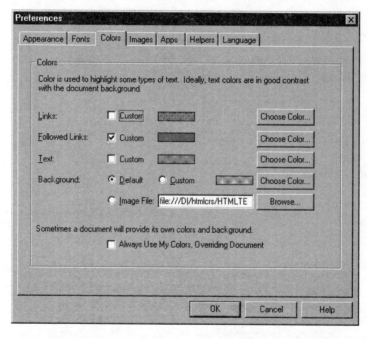

Figure A.1 *General Preferences* dialogue box. Colors tab.

Image File: The file name and path of the image you want displayed as the window background. Click *Browse* to select the file location.

Overriding Document: Check this if you want to prevent a page's background and colours being substituted for your background and colours. By default, the box is unchecked, permitting the background and colours specified by a page's author to be displayed. This should be used with caution otherwise you can destroy any effects the original web page author was trying to achieve.

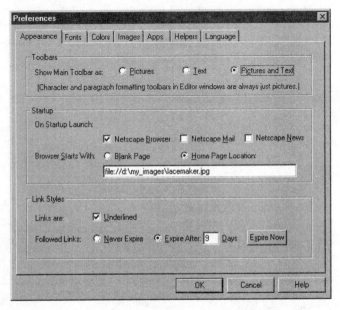

Figure A.2: *General Preferences* - Appearance tab

Most of the settings are self explanatory. But note the *Browser Starts With* section. Choosing *Blank Page* will display a blank page each time you open Netscape.

The *Home Page Location* allows you to enter the location (URL) you want as your startup page. Enter the URL, your own home page, if you wish, in the text field. By default, this field contains the URL of the Netscape application's home page.

Directory
Most of the options are found as buttons on the *Directory Button Bar* unless you have chosen not to show it.

Window
Bookmarks provide a list of your bookmarks in a separate window. (Same as *Go to Bookmarks* in the *Bookmarks* menu.).

History provides a list of the sites visited during a session with the latest page at the top. It provides an easy route back to main web pages rather than using the *Back* button. It also allows you to create a bookmark for any visited site.

Help
Contains the Help reference manual amongst other things.

About is useful if you need to find the version number of your browser.

The Toolbar

The buttons here are self explanatory for the most part. Use the *Back* or *Forward* button to move back and forth amongst pages. This can be cumbersome if you have many pages, in which case you could use the *History* option in the *Window* menu.

The *Home* button takes you back to your home page, the one which Netscape uses when you first call it up. Remember that you can specify a particular home page in the *General Preferences Appearance* tab.

The *Reload* button: Use this if a page looks a bit blotchy. It reloads the web page and removes any distortions. Web authors use this button when they have made changes to a web page and wish to reload the amended version.

The *Images* button: If it is black, then click this button to load any images. If it is grey, images are automatically loaded when the page arrives.

The *Open button:* allows you to type in a URL. Useful if you have chosen to suppress the *Location* toolbar. If you have also suppressed *Toolbar*, then use the *Open* option from the *File* menu.

The *Print & Find* buttons speak for themselves. They are shortcuts to the same options found in the *Menu Bar*.

The Location toolbar

The *Location toolbar* shows the URL of the current web page, for example, your home page when you first call up Netscape. To display some other page, enter its URL in this box, provided you know the correct address, and press the *Enter* key on your keyboard.

The Directory Buttons Bar

What's New: tells you what is new on the Internet.

What's Cool: In Netscape's own words: *"An intriguing page guiding you to the more interesting offerings on the Internet."* But I shall let you be the judge of that!

Netscape Destinations: An exploration page showing you the way to Internet sites and directories. (Very much for the American market.)

Internet Search: A directory of Internet search engines that you can use to find specific information or a particular page, either by searching page titles, subject fields, document content, or other indexes and directories.

People: A directory of services to assist you in locating the names and email addresses of Internet users.

It was somewhat eerie to find my own name on the list (in the top 10 too!).

Software: Lists of Netscape software which you can buy or download for free.

Cache

The first time you ask for a page, Netscape retrieves the page from the network and stores it temporarily on your hard disc, in what it calls a *disc cache* and in the computer's spare memory, the *memory cache*. If you request a page, Netscape checks to see if the page is stored in a cache. For example, if you use the *Back* button to display a page you have already looked at, clicked on a link or a bookmark. Retrieving it again from the cache is quicker than forcing the network to retransmit it.

The memory cache is emptied each time you quit Netscape, but the hard disc is not. Both caches are limited in size and some pages may well be replaced with later ones. In which case, your request for an earlier page has to be sent off to the original server again.

Under the *Options* menu, *Network Preferences* option you can access the following dialogue box. Here you can set the size for both the disc and the memory caches and enter a location for the web cache.

Defaults are established at installation time and the settings are best left alone. Check in the webcache folder to see how much disc space is being taken up.

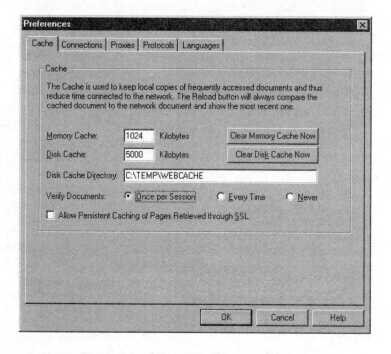

Figure A.3: *General Preferences* - Cache tab

Glossary

advanced searching
techniques by which a large number of hits can be reduced to a more manageable number. These techniques allow users to home in on or narrow their searches to what they really want to find.

BBS
Bulletin Board System. Same as Usenet.

bookmark
a page you wish to visit regularly can be bookmarked. The browser will note the URL address and make a note in its list of bookmarks. The bookmark can be clicked rather than the user having to type in the URL each time.

Boolean operators
words such as AND, OR & AND NOT which can be used to narrow a search list in advanced searching techniques.

boost
a term used by search service providers which increases the relevancy of a Web page which relates to a user's search query.

bots
see crawler.

browser
an application program, such as Netscape or Internet Explorer, which enables you to search the WWW for information and display it on your PC.

cache
in the context of browsers, and pronounced "cash", a temporary storage area in the computer memory or on the hard disc which holds the most recently-downloaded Web pages. As you link from page to page on the Web, caching those pages in memory lets you quickly go back to a page without having to download it from the Web again.

channels
also called *Web guides*. Indexed web pages related to specific topics, e.g. autos, finance, games, health, travel.

concept matching	a technique whereby words entered in a search query are matched in context with other similar words. For example, *elderly* could be matched with *senior citizen*, *OAP*, etc. See also ICE below.
crawler	a jargon term for a search engine.
directories	a search facility whose index of Web pages are categorised by human beings rather than by computer programs.
domain name	that part of a URL which provides the address of a server on the Internet.
frame	where a web screen is divided into two or more sections or separate windows. Typically, clicking on a link in one frame, will display the contents in another without the first being altered.
hierarchies	another term for directories.
hits	in this text, a term meaning the number of returned Web pages which match a user's search query.
home page	the default page retrieved when accessing a Web site. It often serves as a table of contents to the rest of the pages on the site or to other Web sites.
HTML	the languages used to create pages for the WWW.
ICE	Intelligent Concept Extraction. A technology used by Excite to match users' query keywords to similar concepts.
index	in this text, the database of Web pages compiled by search providers and which are queried to find matches to words used to define a topic to be searched for.
ISPs	Internet Service Providers. Commercial companies who provide access to the Internet at a fee.

JavaScript	a language, which has little to do with the Java programming language. It is embedded in Web pages to perform certain functions desired by Web authors.
keyword queries	words and phrases typed in by users when they want to find information.
keywords	in this text, words entered by users to specify what they are looking for.
LAN	Local Area Network. A collection of computers linked together to exchange information. They are usually confined to a building or campus.
link	in this text, it refers to hypertext links which when clicked call up other Web documents.
lists	in this text, the list of returned Web pages in response to a user's query search.
location box	a box provided by browsers into which a URL can be typed. Not to be confused with a *search box* which is used for entering search keywords.
marquee	sites listed by portals in prominent positions on their Web pages in order to advertise them but not so prominently as premier clients.
meta-search engines	service providers who do not own their own database index of Web pages, but forward requests made by their users to many different search tools. The user has access to a larger number of databases than if one search engine or directory were used.
mirror sites	alternate sites which contain the same information as a main site and are usually set up in different States or continents.
nanny software	A program designed to screen out Web sites that feature pornography and other material not suitable for young children and teenagers. See Chapter 12.
newsgroups	another term for Usenet.

portals	a term used to describe a provider who offers more than just simple searching on the Web. They include access to special databases devoted to specific topics, such as travel, jobs, entertainment, buying and selling cars.
premier	sites listed by portals in highly prominent positions on their Web pages in order to advertise them.
protocol	rules governing transmitting and receiving of data between the different operating systems. `http://` & `ftp` & `news:` are some of the ones used.
ranking	techniques used by search providers to list hits of returned matches in an order of relevancy.
robots	see crawler.
router	a device which routes data packets from one local area network (LAN) or wide area network (WAN) to another. Routers often serve as an Internet backbone, interconnecting all networks in the enterprise.
search button	a browser's icon button which when clicked displays a search page enabling users to type in their search queries.
search engines	a computer program which crawls various sites, reading the home pages and following links to other pages. It compiles a list of keywords and URLs and returns them to its database index.
search box	a box provided by browsers and search tools into which you type your query keywords.
search page	a web page which allows users to find information by entering queries into a search box. Because the service is free, these search pages are cluttered up with adverts for other companies and products.

search providers	companies who provide access to their index or database of Web pages compiled either by search engines or directories.
search tools	in this text, any one of several searching facilities, search engines, Web guides, directories, etc.
search trees	another term for directories.
server	in this text, a computer in a network of computers which is shared by multiple users. For example, a computer which maintains and stores all the Web documents at the site.
source code	a term applied to a web document which shows the HTML codes inserted by the Web author.
spamming	in the context of search engines, Web authors enter the same word many times in the hope that the page may be put in a top list of matches.
spider	see crawler.
stop words	certain words which if entered into a search query are totally ignored by the search tool. for example, *the*, *web*, *html*.
subscribe	in the context of newsgroups, joining in a discussion group. There is no payment involved.
thread	a topic or theme in a newsgroup discussion which generates on-going e-mail from interested parties.
traffic	the volume of people who visit a site to request Web pages.
TV set top boxes	devices which can be attached to TV sets and provide a link to the WWW.

URL	the address of where a document is held. It contains the protocol used to communicate between different operating systems and the site address. Frequently the document required forms part of the address.
Usenet	Users Network - a discussion forum for people wishing to exchange ideas. Also called newsgroups.
WAN	Wide Area Network - a communications network that covers a wide geographic area, such as a state or country.
Web author	someone who creates and designs a page for viewing on the Web.
Web Guides	also called *channels*. Indexed web pages related to specific topics, e.g. autos, finance, games, health, travel.
Web master	someone in charge of a LAN web site. He/she maintains the web pages held on the site server.
white pages	directories containing names and addresses of people.
WWW	World Wide Web.
yellow pages	directories containing names and addresses of businesses.

Index